modern

indian literature

a panoramic glimpse

modern indian literature

a panoramic glimpse

krishna kripalani

CHARLES E. TUTTLE COMPANY
Rutland, Vermont & Tokyo, Japan

Representatives
Continental Europe: BOXERBOOKS, INC., *Zurich*
British Isles: PRENTICE-HALL INTERNATIONAL, INC., *London*
Australasia: PAUL FLESCH & CO., PTY. LTD., *Melbourne*
Canada: M. G. HURTIG LTD., *Edmonton*

Published by the Charles E. Tuttle Company, Inc.
of Rutland, Vermont & Tokyo, Japan
with editorial offices at
Suido 1-chome, 2-6, Bunkyo-ku, Tokyo, Japan

© *1971 by Charles E. Tuttle Co., Inc.*

All rights reserved

Library of Congress Catalog Card No. 74-116489

International Standard Book No. 0-8048-0924-0

First edition published in 1968 in the English language
by Nirmala Bhatkal for the Nirmala Sadanand Publishers, Bombay

First Tuttle edition published 1971

0298-000275-4615
PRINTED IN JAPAN

to

one who is no more

contents

The era of modern Indian literature began around the year 1800, when the East India Company established the Fort William College in Calcutta to provide instruction to its British civil servants in the laws, customs, religions, and languages of the country as a systematic measure to meet the increasing demands of a fast-growing civil administrative machinery.

It seems clearly evident that it was the impact of the secular learning and science of the West that was responsible for the intellectual and social turbulence, the revitalization of the spirit that ushered in the modern age.

However dramatic the transition may seem in retrospect, it came noiselessly, with stealthy steps unheard even by those who were paving the way for it. All the while history—or what Tagore invoked, in what is now India's national anthem, as the *Bharata-bhagya-vidhata* (dispenser of India's destiny)—was working out her own mysterious purpose. Many foreigners deserve credit for sparking this spirit, but their work could hardly have borne fruit had it not been for the wholehearted cooperation of a large number of Indian scholars, many of whom were content to remain nameless.

This is not a learned thesis. It claims no merit as a work of original research. Nor is it an essay in creative writing. It is merely an invitation to the general reader to make a panoramic survey of modern Indian literature as a whole, to see how the many languages and literatures of India fit into a common, albeit complex, pattern. If this modest attempt does help to show how Indian literature is one though written in many languages, it will have served its purpose.

The assessment offered in these pages is, at best, tentative. The author does not pretend to a direct and first-hand knowledge of all the languages and literatures covered in this survey. Many evaluations are derived from others and are thus second-hand. If one were a linguistic prodigy and knew well all the languages of our country, even then such a person's literary sensibility and insight may not extend over the whole range. What one truly understands and thus makes one's own is indeed very limited; the rest is mere information culled here and there. Much of what is given in this little volume may be said to belong to the latter category.

Author

One of the oldest literatures of the world, Indian literature in its modern phase is comparatively young and green. The ancient specimens in the *Rig Veda* (about B. C. 1500, if not earlier) are acknowledged as the earliest surviving literary document of Indo-European speech. And yet nothing in these hymns—their language, metrical composition or thought-content—is primitive. This would suggest many centuries of prior literary development before the racial memories, tribal aspirations, the varied experience and imagination of an adventurous and pastoral people could achieve such masterly expression.

To this very ancient lineage must be added some other remarkable features which give its unique character to Indian literature as a whole. One is the almost unbroken continuity of its literary tradition over a period of more than 3000 years. The second is the still surviving vitality of the ancient in the modern. The Vedas, the Upanishads, the Epics, not to speak of the many later Puranas, are much more than mere verbal specimens or literary curiosities to be exhibited in a cultural museum; they are still active sources of inspiration to a large number of people, in life as in letters. One may put it this way : If Homer were not taught in Western schools and universities, the Greek epics would hardly be known outside Greece except to a few academic coteries. In fact, even as it is, it is doubtful if the average European or American who has not had the advantage of a public school or university education can name, much less describe, half a dozen characters from each of the two great Homeric epics. In India, on the other hand, though the *Ramayana* and the *Mahabharata* are hardly ever used as texts in schools and colleges, their main stories and characters are vividly real to most people, young or old.

What is old is not necessarily good, and age by itself need confer no privilege. Nonetheless, it is true that what survives the ravage of time and the caprice of fashion must have an inner vitality, even if it lacks any other validity. And vitality is in itself a virtue, independent of good and bad.

Like the Indian civilisation of which it is more or less a faithful expression, Indian literature is a composite growth reflecting the impact of diverse ages, races, religions and influences, and maintaining simultaneously, sometimes in harmony, sometimes disharmony, different levels of cultural consciousness and intellectual development.

The term 'Indian Literature' is likely to be misleading unless it is understood in almost as broad a sense as the term 'European Literature'. Although

India is one nation and one state the bewildering variety of its languages and literatures rivals that of Europe. A letter from Sarojini Naidu to Jawaharlal Nehru, dated 13 November, 1937, written from Mahatma Gandhi's camp in Calcutta, begins thus : 'I am writing from the modern version of the Tower of Babel. The Little Man is sitting unconcernedly eating spinach and boiled marrow while the world ebbs and flows about him breaking into waves of Bengali, Gujarati, English and Hindi . . .' * It is not an uncommon thing to find in an Indian home the parents conversing with each other in one tongue, talking to their children in another, addressing the servants in a third, and entertaining guests and visitors in yet another and perhaps more than one tongue.

It is more so today than ever, but perhaps it was always so to some extent. It is doubtful if at any period in the recorded history of India the standard or popular medium of communication or of literary expression was confined to one language only. Apart from the fact that there were at least three speech-families already active in the field—the *Nishada* or Austric, *Kirata* or Sino-Tibetan, and Dravidian—when the Aryans came to India, their own Vedic speech soon bore a large progeny. The Dravidians claim for their speech an antiquity which almost rivals that of Sanskrit, and it is conceivable that when the Aryan sages were discoursing in Sanskrit by the shore of the Ganges, the

---

* *A Bunch of Old Letters*, Asia Publishing House, Bombay, 1958.

Tamil poets were composing secular love lyrics on the banks of the Cauvery, while the Buddhist and Jain evangelists turning their back on the literary medium of the learned Brahmins were preaching their gospel in the spoken dialects of the people.

Indian literature has thus always presented a panorama rather than a scene. One has to look around and up and below, to see its many landscapes in proper perspective. If India is a land of contrasts, of sweltering heat and perennial snow, of fabled ease and brutalising want, of the wisdom's calm and the clamour of ignorance, so is its literature many-faced, many-voiced, here primitive, there sophisticated, now inspired, now imitative, at once sublime and grotesque, exhilarating and trite. It is not easy to answer the question : What is modern Indian literature like? It is like literature anywhere else, and it is like literature nowhere else. A pantheon of many gods, with some of the gods many-headed and many-armed.

When the Constitution of India was being framed after independence, the question arose, which of the many current languages should be officially recognised as the major languages of the country. Fourteen such languages were finally thus scheduled : ten of them of Indo-Aryan origin, that is, Sanskrit with its nine progeny, Assamese, Bengali, Gujarati, Hindi, Kashmiri, Marathi, Oriya, Punjabi and Urdu; and four Dravidian—Kannada, Malayalam, Tamil and Telugu. This list is not without its anomalies, for Sanskrit is a 'major' language in quite a different sense from, say, Hindi, Tamil or Bengali, which are living speeches of several million people, while Sanskrit is no longer a spoken tongue, although more than 2,500 persons entered it as their mother tongue in the 1961 Census. Twelve of these languages are predominant speeches of compact regions; whereas Urdu, like Sanskrit, has no specific zone of its own. It is spoken and written in many different parts, as widely separated as Kashmir and Hyderabad. It is also worth noting that most of these languages are written in different scripts, although they are all, with the exception of Urdu, Kashmiri and Sindhi which are written in a modified form of Perso-Arabic script, originally derived from a common parent-script known as Brahmi which can still be seen on the surviving Asokan pillars.

Sahitya Akademi, which is the National Academy of Letters in India, has, in addition to the fourteen languages mentioned in the Constitution of India, recognised three others as of major literary importance : English, Sindhi and, recently, Maithili. The Akademi's assessment is, in a way, more realistic. English, though not an indigenous language of India, is so widely used by the intelligentsia as a medium of communication and education, as also of literary expression, that it may be deemed to function in fact as a major language. The resolution to recognise English as a language with which the National Academy would be actively concerned in its programme was, in fact, moved by Jawaharlal Nehru at the very first annual convocation of the Akademi over which he presided. Sindhi was recognised later, on representations received from a large number of refugees from West Pakistan who had to leave their homeland behind but still cherished their language which is of Indo-Aryan origin and has a written literature of several centuries.* Maithili was recognised recently, on the recommendation of a Committee

---

* Sindhi has since been included in the Eighth Schedule of the Constitution of India, in addition to the fourteen languages mentioned above.

of Linguistic Experts who were unanimously of opinion that Maithili was structurally an independent language and not a dialect of Hindi, and should, in view of its considerable literary heritage and the number of persons who actually speak it (about 5 million), be recognised as an important language.

These seventeen languages, inclusive of English, may be deemed the languages of major use in modern India. From the strictly philological and pedantic point of view, the number of languages, dialects and sub-dialects, like the creeds and castes in the country, is legion. The 1961 Census has listed several hundred. The number may be increased or decreased according to the significance one attaches to linguistic or phonetic variations, or even the way one chooses to name one's mother tongue.* But whatever the value of such meticulous analysis for the professional philologist, it need not concern us here. Suffice for us to note the opinion of Dr Suniti Kumar Chatterji, a reputed authority on the subject, that of the four speech-families of India, over 70 per cent of the population speak one or the other of the various Indo-Aryan languages, and less than one-third the Dravidian languages, while a little over 1 per cent use the Austric and less than 1 per cent the Sino-

'Bharati was returned by 2,118 speakers of which 2,116 were from Uttar Pradesh. Enquiries showed that the individuals enumerated had given a name of Hindi as Bharati, indicating that it is the language of Bharat, i.e., India. *Census of India 1961,* Volume I.

Tibetan tongues. *

Although the importance of a language is not necessarily to be measured by the number of persons speaking it, the relative strength of numbers is not without its significance. From this point of view Hindi may be recognised as the leading language of the country, claiming as it does the allegiance of about 150 million people. This wide sweep of Hindi is not, however, without its limitations, and might be viewed more as a process than as an accomplished and uncontroverted fact.

The term 'Hindi' is used loosely to cover a number of Middle Indo-Aryan speeches spread over a large area in the northern midlands once known as Madhyadesha. Since about A. D. 1000 these speeches or dialects began to acquire distinct characteristics and to evolve literatures of their own which were partly independent of and partly dependent on the Sanskrit heritage. They were known by their separate names and in their characteristic forms are still so known. There is the Braj-bhasha, the vehicle *par excellence* of medieval Vaishnav lyric and the language of Surdas and Bihari; the Awadhi which gave to 'Hindi' literature its greatest poet, Tulsidas, whose *Ramayana* has been called by Grierson † 'the one Bible of a hundred million people ... the perfect example of the perfect book'; Rajasthani in which is recorded the earliest secu-

---

* Chatterji, S. K., *The Languages and Literatures of India*, Bengal Publishers, Calcutta, 1963.

† Grierson, George A., *The Modern Vernacular Literature of Hindustan*, Asiatic Society, 1889.

lar literature of north India in the form of heroic ballads and in which Mira Bai poured her exquisite songs which are today claimed by both Hindi and Gujarati as part of their literary treasure; Bhojpuri, the mother tongue of the great poet Kabir of the 15th century, although he wrote his poems in a mixed and unconventional medium and evolved a rich and vigorous vocabulary of his own which did not disdain words of Perso-Arabic origin.

The case of Maithili illustrates the historical ambiguity in the position of more than one speech of modern India. Maithili is the language of about 5 million people in north-east Bihar, bordering Bengal, with a very rich literary tradition which in the hands of Vidyapati attained such grace and power in the 15th century that its influence was felt as much in Bengal and Assam as in the western zone and had even penetrated into Nepal. So vivid and rich was this impact that even today Vidyapati is claimed by historians of Bengali literature as one of their galaxy and by historians of Hindi literature as one of theirs. As has been stated earlier, Maithili is now recognised by the Sahitya Akademi as an independent language.

This ambiguity is not so anomalous as it may seem if one considers the close affinity that exists between almost all the languages of Indo-Aryan origin. When in 1916 the Bengali scholar, Haraprasad Shastri, published under the title, *Bauddha Doha O Gan,* a manuscript he had discovered in the State Library of Nepal, containing fragments of abstruse mystic poems supposed to date from the 8th century, he claimed them as the earliest specimens of old Bengali. This claim has since been repeated on behalf of almost every other language of north India, from Assamese in the east to Punjabi in the west. Modern scholarship has now reconciled these claims by identifying the language of these songs as the Apabhramsa stage of Prakrit prior to the clear emergence of these modern languages. Indeed, these languages continued to be known as Prakrits for a long time, and early Bengali writers of as late as the 16th century not unoften described their language as Prakrit.

However, whatever be the correct philological status, the fact remains that Bengali and Hindi, as indeed Assamese and Oriya, are the richer for whatever legacy they have derived from Maithili.

In any case, what is known as Hindi today has a vast and varied heritage behind it, though in its present standardised literary form it is of comparatively recent origin, not earlier perhaps than the first decade of the 19th century. It is built on the basic structure of a western Indo-Aryan dialect spoken in and around Delhi and known as Khari Boli (an epithet variously explained but which was perhaps originally derogatory, implying rough, crude or raw speech). In this pristine form it is a very old speech and the famous Persian scholar and poet Amir Khusrau of the 13th century wrote some remarkable verses and riddles in it. He lovingly referred to it as 'Hindawi', though it is possible that to him every indigenous language was 'Hindawi'—belonging to Hind, the name originally given to this land by the early Persians. It was this basic form that was adopted by writers in early 19th century to evolve a literary medium that could cope with the demands of modern education and knowledge.

Begun as a tentative experiment about 160 years ago, Hindi has successfully absorbed the multilinear legacy of its varied ancestry and drawing on the almost limitless reserves of Sanskrit has established itself as the standard literary medium of the largest zone in India. This position has been recognised in the Constitution of India which has conferred on it the status of the official language of the Indian Union—without prejudice to the remaining thirteen or fourteen languages scheduled therein, all of which are recognised as national languages of the country.

Among them Urdu is in a class by itself. This colourful and elegant daughter born of the marriage of two different traditions is Indo-Aryan by ancestry, and rests, like Hindi, on the same basic structure of Khari Boli. But nurtured on an exotic literary tradition and having adopted the Perso-Arabic script, it has acquired an individuality of its own, so that Hindi and Urdu in their highly standardised literary forms seem like two different languages—born of the same soil and sharing a common parentage but alienated from each other by wearing different garbs, loaded with different sets of ornaments.

The word 'Urdu' is of Turkish origin which also gave the word 'horde' to the English language. The original Turkish word 'Ordu' meant the army or camp. Ever since the 11th century * when the Muslims invaded India in wave after wave from the northwest, the rulers, whether Afghan, Turk or Mughal, used Persian as the language of the imperial court. Their army, belonging to different races, also spoke the same language or a mixed jargon, mainly Persian with a sprinkling of Arabic and Turkish words, in which rudiments of the local dialects, Punjabi and Khari Boli, began increasingly to infiltrate. The rough, improvised speech thus born of the confluence of many tongues, but mainly Persian and Khari Boli, came to be known as Urdu or camp language.

In course of time it evolved a standard literary form which was first developed in the Deccan of the 15th century where Muslim adventurers had carved out powerful new kingdoms for themselves, and was therefore known as Dakhani. Its early writers were naturally Muslim poets who adopted the Perso-Arabic script to which they were used and who increasingly loaded their language with the vocabulary and other literary paraphernalia, including prosody, borrowed from Persian and to a lesser extent from Arabic.

This literary medium travelled back to the north where under the patronage of the Mughal and later of the Lucknow court and aristocracy it developed a highly urbane, polished and sophisticated form which has made Urdu different in style from every

* Although Sind was overrun by the Arabs nearly three centuries earlier, the rest of India did not feel the impact of Muslim invasion till the 11th century.

other Indian language and given it a character, a vigour and an elegance all its own. The patronage of the court and aristocracy had at one time invested the language with such prestige and glamour that its use was freely adopted by a large number of educated Hindu families of north India in whose hands the language tended to lose its lopsidedness and to maintain a fairer proportion of Sanskrit and native vocabulary. Such was, for instance, the language of families like the Nehrus and Saprus. It is not without significance that the best-known of modern Hindi writers, Premchand, wrote his first stories and novels in Urdu some of which he later rewrote in what is called Hindi proper.

There is thus, besides High Hindi and High Urdu, a large indeterminate zone where the common speech is an unpretentious middle path between the two, known as Hindustani. Hybrid—like many other ways of common life in the country— racy and popular, this is the speech largely used in a majority of Indian films, which fact is indeed the best testimony to its popular appeal. This, too, was the speech which Mahatma Gandhi cherished and which he strove to propagate as the *lingua franca* of the nation, hoping that it would be accepted as a common heritage by Hindus and Muslims alike. But, like so many of his other dreams, the hope survives as a historical memory only.

Today Urdu is the official language of Pakistan and one of the many national languages of India. Literary pedantry and cultural snobbery have combined to sharpen the cleavage between Hindi and

Urdu, and the ill-concealed contempt which the protagonists of both have for their common foster-child has rendered the position of Hindustani so anomalous that the 1961 Census was unable to compile separate statistics for it, a large number of persons describing their mother tongue as Hindi-Hindustani or Urdu-Hindustani or some other permutation.

The relative strength of numbers speaking the various languages of India, as given in the 1961 Census, may be briefly summed up as under (in alphabetical order): Assamese 6.8 million, Bengali 33.8 million, Gujarati 20.3 million, Hindi (excluding Bhojpuri 7.84 million, Magahi 2.8 million, and Rajasthani 12.3 million) 133.4 million, Kannada 17.4 million, Kashmiri 1.9 million, Maithili 5 million, Malayalam 17 million, Marathi 33.2 million, Oriya 15.7 million, Punjabi 10.9 million, Sindhi 1.3 million, Tamil 30.5 million, Telugu 37.6 million, and Urdu 23.3 million. Bengali, Urdu, Punjabi and Sindhi are also the languages of Pakistan, and it is worth noting that the number of people speaking these languages in Pakistan is as large, if not larger, than in India, and in the case of Sindhi much larger.

Such then is the linguistic jigsaw puzzle of modern India. Without a proper perspective of this complex background one is likely to miss the significance of the most Indian characteristic of Indian literature, namely, its multiple personality. It has been said that Indian literature is one, though written in many languages. A faint echo of the famous vedic verse that Truth is One though sages call it by various names. This characteristic permeates not only literature but almost every significant aspect of Indian life and culture.* Hence the hackneyed phrase, 'Unity in diversity', although there is at least as much diversity in our unity as there is unity in our diversity.

* Here is a leaf from Verrier Elwin's diary, dated 19 October 1934: 'Our company of workers now really representative. There are Christians, Hindus, a Brahmin, a Mussalman, Gonds; polygamists, henogamists, monogamists, celibates; polytheists, henotheists, monotheists, theists, animists, pantheists, monists; vegetarians, egg-eaters, rat-eaters, beef-eaters, and those to whom even the dung of the cow is sacred; bacon-eaters and those to whom even the smell of the pig is anathema. How nice it is!

> 'I am akin to all Earth
> by many a tribal sign,
> the aged pig will often wear
> that sad sweet smile of mine.'

— Elwin, Verrier, *Leaves from the Jungle*: Life in a Gond Village, John Murray, London, 1936.

To some extent this multiple character of Indian literature was always there. Even in the heyday of Sanskrit there existed side by side a considerable body of non-conformist writing in Pali, Prakrits and Tamil. Indeed it is this very multiplicity which has given an added importance to Sanskrit as a centripetal force, a unifying link that has helped to maintain the continuity and integrity of Indian civilisation, feeding with its abundant reserves the many streams that have flowed from it or have drawn from it.

While this it has never ceased to do, its paramountcy was challenged and its vitality considerably impaired by the onslaught of Muslim invasions from the 11th century onwards. Since then it had steadily to yield its pride of place as the exclusive fountainhead of national culture in India and to share this privilege with Persian for about eight centuries.

Persian, too, was Indo-Aryan in origin and a distant cousin of Sanskrit, married into a Semitic family whose script it had adopted, along with

Islamic faith. This graceful and melodious language brought with it the refreshing breath of Sufic thought which served as a stimulus to the resurgence of religious consciousness in medieval India, widening the intellectual horizon of Indian poets and thinkers who felt its affinity to the spiritual insight of the Upanishads. Its influence on Indian thought was healthy and liberative, a fact which is amply borne out by a considerable body of Indian literature, from Kabir to Rammohun Roy. It also brought with it a tradition of secular lyric and allegoric narrative which was a much-needed relief from the monotony of the prevailing modes of piety.

Persian still survives as a literary tradition in India and continues to serve as a source of inspiration and influence to Urdu and Kashmiri poetry, and is taught, along with Arabic, in several major universities of the country. But with the eclipse of its prestige as the language of the rulers, its influence has steadily and rapidly declined.

With the consolidation of British power in India in the beginning of the 19th century, the national role of Sanskrit and Persian as languages which overrode the boundaries of regional mother tongues was increasingly shared by English. Apart from its prestige as the language of the new rulers and as almost the sole passport to Government service and public or professional career, English had the historical advantage of coming to India at a time when Sanskrit and Persian had long played out their mission as languages of enlightenment and had become mere custodians of past glory and sanctuaries of orthodoxy. India has had many dark ages in the long course of her history; of them all the latter half of the 18th century was perhaps the darkest. Political chaos had generated a climate of fear and insecurity. Intellectual lethargy and ritualistic bigotry had combined with moral chicanery and predatory greed to proliferate a wilderness of cankerous growth wherein if culture survived at all it was as a few isolated oases in a vast and weedy desert.

English language thus came at a time when all other doors to an enlightened and progressive outlook seemed hopelessly closed. Patriotic Indians of the post-Gandhian era resent the harsh words with which Macaulay, with more conceit than understanding, pooh-poohed the 'pretensions' of oriental learning in his fateful Minute on Educational Policy in India. But it is well to recall that twelve years before Macaulay's Minute, Rammohun Roy, the most enlightened and patriotic Indian of his generation, had pleaded with the Governor-General Lord Amherst for the official sponsoring of English education in the country and had said in his famous letter of 11 December, 1823 that 'the Sanskrit language, so difficult that almost a lifetime is necessary for its acquisition, is well known to have been for ages a lamentable check to the diffusion of knowledge, and the learning concealed under this almost impervious veil is far from sufficient to reward the labour of acquiring it.'

He himself was a prodigious scholar well versed in Sanskrit as well as Persian and Arabic and these languages he never ceased to love. Nor did he wish or ever propose that his countrymen should cease to cultivate them. What he meant was that in the modern age of which he was the earliest herald in India, none of these languages could serve as an adequate source of knowledge, or, as he put it, of 'a more liberal and enlightened system of instruction embracing mathematics, natural philosophy, chemistry, anatomy, with other useful sciences'.

English language was thus voluntarily, and even enthusiastically, acquired by the young intelligentsia of Bengal, and later of other parts of India, fretting under the load of an inhibitive and meaningless discipline of scholasticism and ritual which the traditional learning had come to be. It is significant that the leaders of the orthodox Hindu society in Calcutta who were bitterly opposed to Rammohun Roy's zeal for social reform and who mercilessly vilified him as an apostate and a traitor to his own religion and community were themselves among the sponsors of the first major institution of English learning in India, the Hindu College which later became the nucleus of the Calcutta University and is today known as the Presidency College.

No doubt, there were also those among the orthodox whose pride in their own cultural tradition effectively came in the way of their acquiring the language of the *feringees,* whatever its material inducements. Maulana Abul Kalam Azad has told us in his reminiscences how his father, a learned theologian and scholar of Arabic and Persian, not only refused to learn the language himself but declined to provide facilities for his son's formal schooling in it, and that as late as the early 20th century.*

There were also those who on patriotic and nationalist grounds denounced with bitterness and 'holy' fervour the British Government's decision to 'impose' a foreign language on Indians, though they themselves were no less ambitious to learn it. This bitterness (with its anomaly of denouncing English while acquiring it) has survived and has indeed been reinforced and made more virulent by political passion—until English has been dislodged from its position as the *Official* language and is retained on sufferance as the *Associate* language, while continuing in fact to perform the same service—more or less.

This service, insofar as it was creative, was twofold. Politically it fostered and strengthened the sense of national oneness more fully and more profoundly than had ever happened before in the country's history. With this sense of oneness grew the aspiration to realise the national destiny as an independent State in a democratic framework. The concepts of the nation-state, of constitutionally guaranteed civic and political rights and of equality of status before the law for all citizens, irrespective of family, caste, religion or sex, are a com-

* Azad, Abul Kalam, *India Wins Freedom*, Orient Longmans, Calcutta, 1959.

monplace today, but for the Hindu society, with its agelong commitment to social hierarchy, to assimilate these concepts a century-and-half ago was nothing short of a revolutionary change.

The Muslims had always believed in common brotherhood and equality of all men, at any rate of the Faithful. More so, perhaps, than the Christians. One would have imagined that this faith of theirs would have had a liberating impact on the Hindu consciousness in course of the eight centuries or more during which Hindus and Muslims had rubbed shoulders in India. But in fact it had only driven the Hindus deeper within the shell of their inhibitive ritualism. But when the same idea came, not in the garb of a religious faith that seemed a challenge to their own but as an intellectual conception, a pure idea supported by reason and vindicated by the French Revolution, the American War of Independence, and the success of British political institutions in general, the Hindu intelligentsia not only welcomed it but even discovered its prototype in their own ancient metaphysics.

The feudal ruling class and traditional bourgeoisie, Hindu and Muslim, had sunk into a mental and moral torpor which had well-nigh paralysed all initiative and spirit of inquiry. A dynamic intelligentsia had to take its place if a new age was to dawn. Such an intelligentsia, fostered under the new regime, took to English language readily, impressed by the wonderland of scientific knowledge and technique thus revealed, and charmed by a literature that seemed the more stimulating because so different from their own. It is instructive to recall the testimony of Romesh Chunder Dutt, the distinguished civilian and historian, and himself a product of this early impact which he summed up thus : *

> The conquest of Bengal by the English was not only a political revolution but ushered in a greater revolution in thoughts and ideas, in religion and society. We cannot describe the great change better than by stating that English conquest and English education may be supposed to have removed Bengal from the moral atmosphere of Asia to that of Europe. All the great events which have influenced European thought within the last one hundred years have also told, however feeble their effect may be, on the formation of the intellect of modern Bengal. The Independence of America, the French Revolution, the War of Italian Independence, the teachings of history, the vigour and freedom of English literature and English thought, the great effort of the French intellect in the eighteenth century, the results of German labour in the field of philology and ancient history—Positivism, Utilitarianism, Darwinism—all these have influenced and shaped the intellect of modern Bengal. In the same degree all the great influences which told on the Bengali mind in previous

* Dutt, Romesh Chunder, *Cultural Heritage of Bengal*, 3rd revised edition, Punthi Pustak, Calcutta, 1962.

centuries, the faith of Krishna, the faith of Chandi or Kali, the preachings of Chaitanya, the belief in the truth of Hinduism and the sacredness of the Shastras, the unquestioning obedience to despotic power in all its phases, the faith in the divine right of royalty and in the innate greatness of princes and princesses—all these ancient habits and creeds have exercised feebler and yet feebler influences on the modern Bengali intellect. In habits, in tastes, in feeling, freedom and vigour and patriarchal institutions, our literature therefore has undergone a corresponding change. The classical Sanskrit taste has given place to the European. From the stories of gods and goddesses, kings and queens, princes and princesses, we have learned to descend to the humble walks of life, to sympathise with a common citizen or even a common peasant. From an admiration of a symmetrical uniformity we have descended to an appreciation of the strength and freedom of individuality. From admiring the grandeur and glory of the great, we now willingly turn to appreciate the liberty and resistance in the lowly.

Insofar as this somewhat sweeping generalisation was a fair assessment of the position in 1877 when these lines were written, it was true only of a very limited intelligentsia in the city of Calcutta, the then vanguard of cultural and literary renaissance in India. It was less true of the other major urban centres, and not at all true of the vast majority somnolent in the villages. Nevertheless, the author had honestly and boldly defined the fundamental trends of the modern age in Bengal, despite the contrary trends (active even then), released by powerful counter-movements, led partly by the very people who had helped to usher in the new age. How increasingly active and strong this counter-movement became may be guessed from the fact that the passage quoted above was omitted by the author from the second edition of his book published in 1895.

It is, indeed, true that this great ferment which transformed the Indian society and made possible its leap from the medieval to the modern age would have come in any case in course of time, as it has come to other peoples in other parts of the world. But historical circumstances made English language the active agent of this ferment in India and gave it a unique role in the development of the modern age and its literature. It would be ungracious, if not churlish, to disown this debt.

Strangely enough, the attraction of English language and the knowledge of its literature (and through it of other Western literatures), instead of thwarting the development of Indian languages, have acted as a powerful stimulus. Perhaps it was not strange at all. It was inevitable. And this is the ultimate testimony to the creative nature of this impact, that all the major languages of India were fertilised by this contact and have yielded, some sooner, some later, rich harvests of their own.

This era of modern Indian literature may be said to begin in 1800 when the East India Company established the Fort William College in Calcutta to provide instruction to its British civil servants in the law, customs, religions and languages of the country as a systematic measure to meet the increasing demands of a fast-growing civil administrative machinery. About the same time the Baptist Mission set up a press in Serampore near Calcutta, with the object of propagating the Christian gospel among the 'heathen' population. Whatever the original objects and however sordid colonialism and proselytism may seem today, the actual working of these two institutions produced results far beyond those intended. The credit for this must largely go to the personalities involved, in particular to the missionary zeal and versatility of the indefatigable William Carey, the scholarship and talent of Dr John Gilchrist the dynamic head of the Fort William College, and the learned and devoted band of Indian scholars associated with them, Mritunjaya Vidyalankar, Ram Ram Basu, and others in Bengali, Lalluji Lal and his colleagues in Hindi, Sher Ali Afsos and others in Urdu; and many more.

Whether for training civil servants or for propagating the Gospel, it was necessary to use the spoken languages of the people. But though these languages had had a considerable medieval literature, it was mainly in verse and in a language and style which were far removed from the workaday speech in actual use. A kind of working prose had therefore to be evolved in which textbooks could be written or translations made. What tradition of written prose was there in modern Indian languages or in Sanskrit was not adequate for the utilitarian purpose for which it was now needed. It was too ornate or stylised. As is well known, the Sanskrit poetics made no clear-cut qualitative distinction between poetry and prose, even as it made no such distinction between *belles lettres* and didactic literature. Verse was in no way essential to poetry which might be metrical or in prose or partly verse, partly prose. On the other hand, even grammars and dictionaries were written in verse, and a novel in prose might be little different from a *kavya*. In any case there was hardly any well-established native literary tradition of what we understand by prose today which could be used as an effective medium of mass communication of knowledge or information.

'Whatever remnants of prose,' writes a distinguished historian of Bengali literature, 'we may be able to unearth from old records and manuscripts in order to vindicate the glory of our past literature, it must, for the sake of truth, be admitted that they were too insignificant to deserve prominent mention in a history of literature. Disconnected from the story of the later development of prose that has grown up like a rich harvest during the British rule, they would scarcely deserve more than a passing notice.' *

What is said above of Bengali is true, more or less, of all other Indian languages as well, even though some of them, like Tamil, Kannada, Assamese or Marathi, did have a somewhat ampler record of prose writing. It was in Bengal, however, that the modern age in India dawned—due, no doubt, to an accident of history.

It was also a fortunate accident that the official Government initiative in establishing an academic centre at the Fort William College and the missionary enterprise in setting up the first printing press coincided. The Baptist William Carey was the link between the two and proved to be an inspiring and tireless pioneer. Starting life as a cobbler in his home country he came to Bengal as a missionary and soon made himself a master of more than one Indian language. Besides translating the Bible and writing numerous treatises on Christianity, he compiled, wrote or edited, and published the following in Bengali : a Dictionary of the Bengali Language in 3 volumes comprising 80,000 words, a Bengali Grammar, a *Kathopaka-*

---

* Sen, Professor Dinesh Chandra, *History of Bengali Language and Literature*, University of Calcutta, 1954.

tham or collection of samples of Bengali colloquial speech, and an *Itihasamala* or garland of 150 popular stories current in Bengal. 'The last two books form a rich mine of idioms of the spoken dialect of Bengal from which Tek Chand Thakur took the cue for his style in the composition of his masterpiece in Bengali—*Alaler Gharer Dulal.*' *

Carey was not, however, the first to write a Bengali grammar or to print it. This distinction belongs to Nathaniel Brassey Halhed who wrote the first Bengali Grammar and printed it more than two decades earlier in 1778 in a press at Hooghly. The printing was made possible by the skill and zeal of Charles Wilkins † who was the first to cut Bengali types and to train a local blacksmith, Panchanan Karmakar, in the art and technique of casting type in a foundry. It was Panchanan who was engaged by Carey and his colleagues in the Serampore Mission to run their press and who also made the first matrices of the devanagari letters for Hindi. Assamese and Marathi also owe their first printed books to this press which 'issued between 1801 and 1832 more than two hundred and twelve thousand volumes in forty

* *Ibid.* Besides Bengali, Carey studied and mastered a number of other north-Indian languages and dialects and wrote grammars of Marathi and Punjabi.

† Who was also the first Englishman to acquire a knowledge of Sanskrit. His English translation of *Bhagavat Gita* published in 1785 was the first book translated directly from Sanskrit into a European language.

different languages.' *

The history of the printing press in Southern India is indeed much older. The Jesuit missionaries had set up their press in Goa as early as 1556, and books in Tamil and other Dravidian languages began to be printed since the second half of the 16th century.† Many foreign missionaries learnt the languages of the people and not only translated the Bible and wrote Christian *Puranas* in them but rendered undying service to the languages by preparing and compiling the first modern grammars and dictionaries. The pioneer labour of the German missionary Ziegenbalg † † and his Italian successor Beschi in Tamil, and of Father Leonardo Cinnoma in Kannada as well as of many others in Telugu and Malayalam is still recalled with gratitude in the histories of these literatures.

But although the printing press came to south India much earlier and the foreign missionary enterprise functioned much longer and more zealously than in Bengal, the creative impact of Western thought as such made itself felt much more slowly and the resurgence of literary spirit bore

* Brochure published by the National Library. Calcutta, 1956.

† 'The first printing in Indian characters was said to be done at Ambalakkadu in Cochin where the first "Malabar" types were cut by Joannes Gonsalvez in 1577. However, it has not been possible to trace in India any of these books.'—*Ibid.*

† † He cut the founts of Tamil type and published the first Tamil translation of the New Testament in 1715.

fruit in its modern form much later than in Bengal. A clear evidence that it was the impact of the secular learning and science of the West made available through education in the English language and not Christianity or the mere technique of printing that was responsible for the intellectual and social turbulence, the churning of the spirit that ushered in the modern age.

However dramatic the transition may seem today in retrospect, it came noiselessly, with stealthy steps unheard even by those who were paving the way for it. The East India merchants and their henchmen were pleased that they were consolidating their framework of commercial exploitation and political subjugation; the missionaries were pleased that they were saving heathen souls for the glory of Christendom. All the while History— or what Rabindranath Tagore invoked in what is now India's national anthem as the *Bharata-bhagya-vidhata* (Dispenser of India's destiny)— was working out her own mysterious purpose. Nonetheless, all credit to those who were her instruments, conscious or unconscious. Among them will live the names of many foreigners, William Jones, Charles Wilkins, Nathaniel Halhed, William Carey and his colleagues Dr Marshman and Dr Ward at Serampore, Dr John Gilchrist of the Fort William College and others. Their work, however, could hardly have borne fruit if they had not received the unstinted cooperation of a large number of Indian scholars many of whom were content to remain nameless.

But the most creative spirit among the early pioneers, foreign or native, and one who knowingly sought and anticipated the modern age and may therefore be said to be the first consciously dedicated instrument of the *Bharata-bhagya-vidhata* was Raja Rammohun Roy (1772-1833). He laid the true foundation of modern Bengali prose, as indeed he did of the Indian awakening in general. Though essentially a religious and social reformer, the learning, versatility and untiring zeal of this remarkable man blazed new trails in almost every field of Indian life and culture. He wrote and published (at his expense) 27 works in Bengali, among them translations of the Upanishads,* textbooks, a Bengali grammar, religious and social tracts, etc. As to his contribution to the development of Bengali language, the following testimony of a distinguished authority is worth quoting:

We repeat that it would have been impossible for any other man of his age, however learned, to have reduced such great and abstruse truths (of the Upanishads) to pristine simplicity in a lan-

* The first ever done. Rammohun also presented to the world, through his English rendering, the first translation of the Upanishads done directly from the original Sanskrit into any European language. The earlier translation which had reached Europe and to which Schopenhauer had referred so lyrically was through a Latin translation (*Oupnek'hat*) by a French scholar from Dara Shikoh's Persian rendering of the 17th century.

guage which as yet was so inadequate to the purpose as our own. It was possible for the Raja to do so only because he was himself a seer of these truths like the great sages—the Rishis of the past...

The Bengali grammar written by the Raja, though a short treatise, bears the impress of his great genius.... He observed the genius of our language, and in what respects it differed from Sanskrit; he formulated principles based on the natural laws which govern Bengali, and treated the subject scientifically.*

It was fortunate that Rammohun Roy had worthy successors who could build on the foundation laid by him—Debendranath Tagore (Rabindranath's father, known as the Maharshi or the Great Sage), Aksay Kumar Datta (1820-86) who ably edited the journal *Tattva-bodhini Patrika* founded by the Maharshi, and above all and particularly so far as the development of Bengali prose is concerned, Iswar Chandra Vidyasagar (1820-91) who had begun his early career as a Pundit in Fort William College and in whose hands the Bengali prose attained a maturity and dignity unknown before. All three of them were, like their great predecessor, primarily social reformers and educationists. And because they were men of high purpose who had much to say, they had little use for rhetoric and flamboyance otherwise natural to a language derived from Sanskrit. They succeeded

* Sen, Professor Dinesh Chandra, *op. cit.*

in chiselling a prose at once chaste and vigorous.

Path-makers rather than creative artists, they standardised the medium which their younger contemporary, Bankim Chandra Chatterji (1834-94), turned with superb skill and gusto into a magnificent tool for his novels and stories. Bankim Chandra is known as the father of the novel in India. Fables, stories and tales of romantic adventure had been known to India for more than two thousand years, but the novel, as the term is understood today, is a Western importation. Bankim's genius made the alien form native, which explains his influence, profound and extensive, on his contemporaries and successors.

Novels, both historical and social, the two forms in which he excelled, had been written before him in Bengali by Bhudev Mukherji and Peary Chand Mitra. Mitra's *Alaler Gharer Dulal* published under the author's pen-name Tek Chand Thakur is indeed the first specimen of original fiction as well as of social realism in Bengali, with (moreover) free use of the colloquial idiom, and may be said to have anticipated, however crudely, the later and post-Bankim development of the novel.* Nevertheless, it was Bankim Chandra who established the novel as a major literary form in India. He had his limitations, he was too romantic, effusive and

---

* Mitra's work, though in a sense more modern than Bankim's, was so overshadowed by the latter's superior genius that it had little impact on his contemporaries. His only follower was Kaliprasanna Sinha whose *Hutom Pyanchar Naksha* was modelled on the earlier novel.

didactic, he indulged a little too freely in literary flourishes and bombast, and was no peer of his great European contemporaries, Balzac and Dickens, much less of Tolstoy and Dostoevsky. There have been better novelists in India since then, but they all stand on Bankim's shoulders.

Thus prose led the way in this new march from the medieval to the modern. This was as it should be, since prose is the backbone of modern literature all the world over. But poetry did not lag behind and its achievement soon overtook its pedestrian rival. And no wonder. Apart from the fact that the tradition of poetry was always strong in India as a whole, the Bengali temperament is particularly susceptible to its appeal, and being emotional, its responsiveness to new influences is quick and sensitive. The Bengali language, too, is supple and musical, as though fashioned for lyrical expression.

And yet it was with an epic and not with a lyric, with a bang rather than with a whimper, that the new era in poetry announced itself.

Michael Madhusudan Dutt (1824-73) made the first successful experiment, and a gigantic one at that. He wrote the first modern epic in an Indian language and naturalised blank verse in Bengali. His personal life was a tragic struggle to justify Western values in an Indian context, but the fusion he vainly sought to achieve in life he accomplished in poetry with a success which won for him an everlasting name in Indian literature. But though he led the way, he could not establish a vital tradition, for his own success was a *tour de force* of an erratic genius.

His contribution has been well summed up by a distinguished scholar : * 'To his adventurous spirit we owe blank verse and the sonnet, our first modern comedy and tragedy, and our first epic. He is the pioneer of our new (i.e., westernised) poetry and our new drama. The heroic note he introduced into Bengali poetry gave it a power and weight, a richness and elevation, it never had before. In his *Meghnadvadh* and *Virangana* the rustic Bengali muse spoke the language of Valmiki and Vyasa, as well as of Homer, Tasso, and Milton. In introducing blank verse he gave to Bengali poetry a music that was as rich as it was novel; with almost miraculous skill he elicited from the dulcet-toned Bengali *vina* the deep notes of the Miltonic organ.†

* Ghosh, J. C., *Bengali Literature*, Oxford University Press, London, 1948.

† Considering how little is Milton appreciated or even read in India today, it is remarkable how the early pioneers of modern Indian poetry were both impressed and inspired by him. In one of his letters Madhusudan wrote: 'Nothing can be better than Milton... I don't think it impossible to equal Virgil, Kalidas and Tasso. Though glorious, they are still mortal poets. Milton is divine.' More than forty years later, the Urdu poet Iqbal, a leading exponent of Islamic thought, wrote to a friend in 1903: 'For a long time I have been yearning to write in the manner of Milton (*Paradise Lost*. etc.) and the time for that seems to be fast approaching, because in these days there is hardly a moment, when I am not thinking seriously of this.' (Quoted

'He is the earliest, and the greatest, product of Western influence, and represents in his life and work both its happy and its unhappy aspects ... The East and the West no doubt meet with many happy results in his work, but they also meet superficially ... His is the tragic case of a man who had his head in India and his heart in England, and who fell between two worlds, the East and the West. But for that fundamental disunity in his consciousness he might have been a far greater poet and a happier man.'

'This fundamental disunity' is perhaps the price that a great pioneer must pay who has to lead his age from one tradition to another. Michael Madhusudan could hardly have achieved what he did, if he had not been an ardent admirer of European literature and a passionate lover of his own language. 'I would sooner reform the poetry of my country,' he wrote to a friend, 'than wear the diadem of all the Russians.'

in *Iqbal, His Art and Thought* by Sayed Abdul Vahid, Shaikh Md. Ashraf, Lahore, 1944.)

While the credit of introducing Western forms into Indian literature belongs to his eminent predecessors, it was Rabindranath Tagore who made Indian literature truly modern in its own right. Bankim Chandra indeed succeeded in naturalising the novel as a popular form of modern Indian literature, but though great as a pioneer he soon ceased to be a good model. Today a novelist who wrote like him would hardly be read. His eminence is historical rather than universal, and his continued legendary popularity rests at least partly on the fact that he was at heart a passionate nationalist and somewhat of a Hindu revivalist. Which is why he was far more popular with his readers whose romantic vainglory and sentimental bias he reflected in a glorified image than Tagore who, because he was truly modern and therefore ever surpassing himself and always ahead of his contemporaries, was an isolated and lonely figure. Michael Madhusudan Dutt, too, was lonely and isolated, but in a very different way. He was at heart alienated, and more a European than an Indian, hanging tragically between two worlds to neither of which he could belong.

Though indebted to both Bankim and Michael, Rabindranath Tagore's genius was of a different order. He achieved success not by a forced adaptation of foreign models or by ministering to popular sentiments, but by his own uniquely creative response to the impulse of the age. He made no herculean effort to pour Indian contents into Western moulds, but let himself browse freely and without compulsion or inhibition on whatever suited his genius—on the classical, medieval and folk traditions of his own land and on whatever foreign pasture came his way, with the result that the reflective grandeur of the Upanishads, the chaste sensuousness of Kalidasa, the lyrical abandon of Vaishnav devotion, and the rustic virility of the folk idiom are so well blended with Western influences in his poems and songs, his stories and dramas, that generations of academic pundits will continue to wrangle over his specific debt to each or any of them. In him modern Indian literature came of age and attained its true stature—not only in poetry but in prose as well. He was so well rooted in his homely native soil that he drew his deepest inspiration not so much from the classical Indian or the Western European as from the indigenous folk heritage. Above all it was the landscape of his native Bengal, its earth and sky, its change of seasons, its familiar sights and sounds, the humdrum lives of the simple, common people that provided the main sustenance of his work as a creative writer. 'He is the most Indian of the Indian poets as well as the most universal.' *

* Sen, Dr Sukumar, *History of Bengali Literature*, Sahitya Akademi, New Delhi, 1960.

Like poetry in Madhusudan's hands and the novel in Bankim's, the modern drama too owed its first flowering to foreign grafting. The tradition of classical Sanskrit drama had long been lost and had not, in any case, percolated the popular pattern of culture. But drama is life and there is hardly a people who do not love to mimick or watch a visual representation, realistic or symbolic, of their life and lore, and so a kind of composite folk drama had grown up in varying forms all over India—Kathakali in Malabar, Yakshagana in Karnataka, Ankiya Nat in Assam, Tamasha in Maharashtra, Yatra in Bengal, Khayal in Rajasthan, Ras-lila in Braj and Manipur, Ramlila in the Gangetic plain, and so on. In them Pauranic themes as well as legendary and popular lore were represented on an improvised stage with the help of dialogue, declamation, mime, song and dance. This crude but delicious hotchpotch of song, drama and dance, of the sacred and the profane, is even to-day more popular with the masses than what is known as drama proper which is essentially an urban growth and a cultivated and sophisticated art requiring considerable organisation and resources.

Calcutta had grown as the first cosmopolitan city in India under the new foreign regime. It was thus natural that it should witness the birth of modern imported drama. (Calcutta has continued to retain the liveliest stage tradition in India.) Curiously enough, the first stage-play produced in Bengali in Calcutta was by a Russian adventurer-cum-indologist, Lebedev, in 1795. It was an adaptation of a little-known English comedy, *The Disguise,* by Richard Jordell, oddly interspersed with English and Hindustani dialogue to suit the needs of a mixed audience. The main dialogue, however, was in Bengali, and the actors and actresses were likewise Bengali.

Many years passed before a serious attempt was made to build an authentic stage, mainly under private patronage. The first original play in Bengali was *Kulin Kulasarvasva,* a social satire against the practice of polygamy among Kulin Brahmins, written by Pandit Ramnarayan. When Ramnarayan's second play, *Ratnavali,* based on a Sanskrit classic, was about to be staged at a private theatre under the patronage of two local Rajas or landed magnates, Madhusudan Dutt was requested to render it into English so that the Rajas' English friends might follow the action on the stage. What a pity, remarked Madhusudan to a friend at one of the rehearsals, that the Rajas should waste so much good money over so poor a play! When the friend pointed out that there were hardly any good plays in Bengali, the impetuous poet replied, Why, I shall write one. Thus Madhusudan wrote his first play, *Sarmistha* (based on a story from the *Mahabharata)* in 1858, and became, almost by accident, a Bengali writer. 'It is not a good play, but is important as the first Bengali work by Madhusudan and as the first Bengali play to be constructed in the modern Western style.' *

He wrote a few more plays in quick succession, one of them based on the Greek legend of Paris and the apple of discord, another on a tale of Rajasthan told by Todd, as well as some satirical farces. Although he may thus be said to have laid the foundation of modern Indian drama, as he did of poetry, his achievement as a dramatist did not equal his performance as a poet, and he soon retired from the adventure to take up a bigger challenge in the arena of poetry. He was essentially a poet and not a dramatist, and he had hardly any respect or feeling for the dramatic tradition of his own land. 'The genius of the Drama,' he wrote in a letter, 'has not yet received even a moderate degree of development in this country.'

His place was taken by lesser geniuses who were on the whole better dramatists. Dinabandhu Mitra (1829-74) has an assured place in the history of Indian drama as being the first to use drama for exposing a major economic evil of the day, namely, atrocities of the British indigo-planters. The play he wrote on it, *Nil Darpan* (1860), created a sensation as much political as literary. The Rev. J.

* Ghosh, J. C., *op. cit.*

Long, a brave missionary who had the audacity to publish an English translation of it done by Madhusudan Dutt (anonymously), was fined and jailed by the British authorities. * This play has also the distinction of being the first with which the public theatre opened in Calcutta in 1872. Mitra wrote several other plays including farces but he is best remembered as the author of *Nil Darpan*.

He was followed by a succession of playwrights among whom the most notable for their popularity and success on the stage were Girish Chandra Ghosh (1844-1911) and Dwijendra Lal Roy (1863-1913). The former, actor-director-playwright, who wrote and produced about eighty plays, is the real founder and populariser of the public stage in Calcutta. But though both he and D. L. Roy achieved phenomenal popularity in their day, the public appeal owed more to the patriotic, pseudo-religious and melodramatic elements in their plays than to any abiding literary or even dramatic, as distinguished from theatrical, merit.

The only truly creative and original dramatist of modern India was Rabindranath Tagore, but his plays, mainly symbolic and at once mystic and intellectual in the true Indian tradition, proved too subtle and elusive for the contemporary taste which had been debased by crude adaptation or

---

* Even the then Viceroy, Lord Canning, was constrained to admit that the High Court judgment had displayed indecent partisanship'.—Gopal, S., *British Policy in India 1858-1905*, Cambridge University Press, 1965.

imitation of Western realism or cruder revival of indigenous melodrama to suit the emergent patriotic sentiments. And so he too failed to establish a firm tradition in the field, with the result that of all literary forms in modern Indian literature the drama remains the least developed.*

---

* Recent experiments of the talented actor-director Sombhu Mitra and his Bohurupee Theatre in Calcutta have shown how rich is the potential of Tagore drama when properly presented on the modern stage. Here is his own testimony: 'I am reminded of a remark by Annada Sankar Ray (a leading contemporary poet and novelist of Bengal) some years ago. He said theatres in Calcutta were tenth-rate imitations of those in the west. According to him, we must go to Tagore as there was no alternative. The full import of the remark was not quite clear to me at the time . . . . And then we produced *Raktakarabi* (known to English readers as *Red Oleanders*) which was a turning point. Before it we had produced *Chaar Adhyaya* (stage version of Tagore's novel of that name). While working on *Raktakarabi* we slowly discerned an Indian mode of dramatic unity, the blending of the inner and the outer life of the individual and the symbol, etc., within a single frame. It was then that we realised that the Bengali stage could progress only when we took Tagore seriously.' ('The Root of Indian Theatre' by Sombhu Mitra, *The Hindustan Times Weekly*, Sunday, April 24, 1966)

An important reservation to be kept in mind in discussing any aspect of modern India, literary or social, is that it should never be assumed that the modern, however dominant, ever wholly displaced the old. As a matter of fact, even while the Western literary innovations discussed above were being firmly established and had attained a high prestige, the traditional forms continued to be practised and never ceased to have a popular appeal. All through the 19th century the indigenous nomadic theatre, the Yatra of Bengal, continued to be popular—even in Calcutta where the modern theatre was gaining a stronghold. In the country outside Calcutta the Yatra had almost no rival. No modern drama written or produced in Calcutta ever matched the phenomenal popularity of the Yatras composed by the village poet Krishna Kamala whose *Svapnavilas* written in 1835 sold 20,000 copies 'within a few weeks in Eastern Bengal where a demand for printed books had not yet been created.' *

* Sen, Professor Dinesh Chandra, *op. cit.*

The same is true of the popularity of Kaviwallas, professional versifiers who engaged in public contests of extemporised verses. Such was the vogue of this popular literary entertainment that one Mr Antony of Portuguese parentage who had fallen in love with an attractive Brahmin widow turned into a well-known Kaviwalla with a professional troupe of his own. The *Panchalis* (doggerels which are sung) of Dasarathi Rai (1804-1857) were so popular that he could keep an audience entranced the whole night with an endless series of extemporised verses whose main charm lay in their alliteration and punning, their occasional wit and more frequent vulgarity. Here is a specimen: 'Faith adorns a scholar; lightning adorns the cloud; the husband's love adorns a woman; the crops adorn the earth; its own lustre adorns a jewel; the fruits adorn a tree; water adorns a river; the lily adorns the water; the bee adorns a lily; . . .' and so on, verse following trite verse, each greeted with thunderous applause.*

No less relevant and significant is the case of Iswar Gupta (1811-1858) the most important literary figure of the first half of the 19th century. This second-rate poet and brilliant satirist was a minor Pope of his age and dominated the literary scene with his wit and venom. Motherless, brought up in an unhappy home ruled by a step-mother, and married at the age of 15 to an ugly half-witted girl—for no better reason than that she came of a high pedigree, Iswar Gupta's mental outlook was

* *Ibid.*

distorted at an early age, and he grew up to hate and deride anything that seemed to him modern and therefore westernised. He was almost illiterate until one of the Tagores took him under his wing, had him educated and started the weekly *Samvad Prabhakar* for him to edit in 1830. It was in the pages of this journal that the early writings of Aksay Kumar Dutt, Bankim Chandra Chatterji and Dinabandhu Mitra were first published. A better journalist than poet, Iswar Gupta was also the first to write literary biographies of some earlier Bengali poets. This anti-modern provided, ironically, a training ground for some of the architects of the modern age, and illustrates the curious case of blind allegiance to an outworn tradition of which he himself had been a tragic victim.

Historical circumstances aided by emotional sensibility enabled the people of Bengal to react warmly to new influences from outside and gave their language the distinction of leading the way in the march of modernity in India. But the general pattern of literary, as indeed of social and political, resurgence was more or less the same in all the language zones of the subcontinent, each responding in its own fashion, some eagerly, some lukewarmly, some sooner, some later. In almost all of them the early spadework was done by Christian missionaries or British civil servants and foreign indologists who helped to hammer out the basic material on which the development of prose was built. Gradual cross-fertilisation with European literature through English education was made easier by the highly refined spiritual sensibility of the Indian mind cultivated through centuries of cultural interbreeding. This made possible a warm response to the liberal humanist tradition of Western thought. Thus stimulated, and further equipped with the technique of modern research, the Indian mind discovered anew, as it were, the rich treasure of its own ancestral legacy. So deep was the impact of this discovery that as late as 1946 Jawaharlal Nehru named the book in which he surveyed his country's past as *Discovery of India*.

The fact that this literary resurgence was part of a general social and political awakening and was closely linked in its early phase with a quickening of the moral sensibility gave to the movement the creative fervour of a new-born faith in Indian destiny. The crusading zeal and dedicated lives of Raja Rammohun Roy, Maharshi Debendranath Tagore, Iswar Chandra Vidyasagar, Keshav Chandra Sen, Ramakrishna Paramahamsa, and later of Swami Vivekananda and Sri Aurobindo were sources of inspiration, not to Bengal alone but to the whole of India. No wonder the early pioneers of the modern movement in all Indian literatures were most of them also active social reformers and men of outstanding moral stature.

Patriots and humanists, they struggled to free themselves from the fetters of a rigid formalism— what Tagore dramatised as *Achalayatan* (citadel of immobility)—and to build new paths towards an unknown destiny. Beneath the debris of what seemed the dead past they discovered a great heritage. The first light was borrowed from the West, but very soon the sun arose on the eastern horizon. Discovery of the ancient heritage was in a sense a partial recovery and became an inspiration as well as a burden, at once a spur and a shackle. Henceforth the march ahead was never uninhibited—always hesitant, interrupted by lingering looks behind.

It is hardly necessary to clutter this short survey with a catalogue of names. A few particularly significant ones may, however, be noted in passing.

Marathi was, after Bengali, the most vigorous in its response to the challenge of the new age—partly because of its own robust intellectual tradition sharpened by memories of an erstwhile glory of the Maratha empire, and partly because Bombay, like Calcutta, provided a cosmopolitan background and stimulus. Among the stalwarts who laid the foundation of its modern literature may be mentioned the poet Keshavsut whose birth-centennial was celebrated in 1966, the novelist Hari Narayan Apte born a year earlier, and Agarkar, Chiplunkar and Rajwade who hammered and chiselled the modern Marathi prose. Apte's novels stimulated the development of modern fiction in some other neighbouring languages, particularly in Kannada. Kirloskar and Deval did for the Marathi stage what Girish Chandra Ghosh had done for the Bengali. Narmad's poetry blazed the trail in Gujarati, while Goverdhanram's *Saraswati-*

chandra marked a turning point in fiction and still remains a landmark.

The development of modern Assamese and Oriya, the two eastern neighbours of Bengali, was somewhat late in coming on account of political and historical handicaps. Its advent, too, was preceded by valuable spadework done by Christian missionaries.* Assam was torn by civil strife in the 18th century, and was later invaded and occupied by Burma until the British rescued and annexed it in 1827. Orissa, for long mutilated and dismembered, recovered its homogeneity rather late in the present century. The intelligentsia of both the regions were educated in Calcutta (which was then the main educational centre in eastern India) and carried back with them an impact of the literary resurgence they had witnessed there. Lakshmikanta Bezbarua, Padmanath Gohain Barua and Rajanikanta Bardoloi ploughed the virgin fields and garnered the first fruits of modern poetry,

---

* The remarkable contribution of Christian missionaries, Carey and Marshman of Serampore, as well as of the American Baptist Mission has been ably discussed and assessed by Dr Birinchi Kumar Barua in his *History of Assamese Literature*, Sahitya Akademi, 1964. As regards the advent of the British in Orissa, Dr Mayadhar Mansinha in his *History of Oriya Literature* (Sahitya Akademi, 1962) relates: 'When the British occupied Orissa in 1803, the priests of the Temple of Jagannatha could welcome their victorious general in sonorous, adulatory Sanskrit, because the 200 years under the rule of the Moghuls, the Pathans and the Marathas had created completely anarchical conditions in the country.'

drama and novel in Assamese. In Oriya the nove-list Fakirmohan Senapati, the poets Radhanath Roy and Madhusudana Rao laid the early foundation of the modern period.

The development of Hindi prose, along with Bengali, at the beginning of the 19th century, has already been referred to. 'It was the period of the birth of the Hindi language,' remarked G. A. Grierson, 'invented by the English, and first used as a vehicle of literary prose composition in 1803, under Gilchrist's tuition, by Lallu Ji Lal, the author of the *Prem Sagar*.'* This casual dictum of an erudite and well-meaning scholar is likely to be misunderstood if torn out of its context. Grierson was well aware that Hindi, even in its Khari Boli form on which its modern superstructure rests, can claim a fairly old pedigree. Amir Khusrau (1255-1325), one of the most versatile and accomplished poets of his age, had referred to the language spoken in and around Delhi as 'Hindawi' or 'Dehlavi', in which he had himself composed many verses which even today sound as charming and fresh as any written during the 700 years since.† Even as regards prose,

* *op. cit.,*

† Husain, Yusuf, *Glimpses of Medieval Indian Culture*, Asia Publishing House, Bombay, 1957. The author has cited and translated into English one of Amir Khusrau's verses in 'Hindawi' composed by him at the grave of his spiritual preceptor Shaikh Nizamuddin Auliya which is well worth quoting here:

Gori soe sej par, mukh par dale kes,
Chal Khusrau ghar apne, rain bhai chaudes.

Hindi scholars and historians have cited as specimens 'Gang's small prose treatise on prosody written in 1555 in the spoken dialect of Delhi *(Chand Chhand Barnam ki Mahima)* as also Ram Prasad's *Yog Vasisth* in 1741, and Insha Allah's *Rani Ketki ki Kahani,* written in 1800, which is supposed to be the first novel in Hindi as it is known today'.*

In fairness to Grierson it is well to point out that what he had in mind was not the 'Hindawi' of Amir Khusrau or the language used in the prose treatises of Gang and his successors, but the highly laboured medium consciously cultivated by Pundits of the Fort William College which Grierson described as an 'artificial dialect, the mother tongue of no native-born Indian, a newly invented speech, that wonderful hybrid language known to Europeans as Hindi and invented by them.' There is little doubt that this medium which was primarily needed for the use of the British civil servants had literally to be manufactured.

It was later naturalised by gifted pioneers who were faced with the task of cutting deep and wide the channel of Khari Boli, to transform it into a broad and expansive river-bed into which the waters

(The fair one sleeps on the bed with the tresses scattered on her face. O Khusrau, come home now, for night has fallen all over the world.) Khusrau died shortly after and was buried at the foot of his master's grave. The mausoleum which contains both the graves is still a famous place of pilgrimage in Delhi.

* Jindal, K. B., *A History of Hindi Literature,* Kitab Mahal, Allahabad, 1955.

of many tributaries could flow and which could be perennially fed from the vast reservoir of Sanskrit. This engineering feat which has made modern Hindi what it is was performed by Harischandra (1850-1885), known to a grateful posterity as 'Bharatendu' (Moon of India) for his service to Hindi literature and his public spirit and philanthropy, by Mahavir Prasad Dwivedy (1870-1938), pioneer essayist, and Jaya Shankar Prasad (1890-1937), poet and dramatist who introduced blank verse.

The problem of Urdu, as was stated earlier, was different and in a category by itself. In basic structure the same as Hindi, its style owes its origin and development to an increasing admixture of words of foreign origin, Persian, Arabic and Turkish, and to the influence, mainly, of Persian poetry. It was therefore also known as 'Rekhta', meaning 'mixed'.* Flourishing under the patronage of Muslim rulers, it developed rapidly from the 15th century onwards, first mainly in the Deccan where it had powerful patrons in the Qutub Shahi rulers of Golconda and the Adil Shahi kings of Bijapur. Sultan Md. Quli Qutb Shah, fourth king of the dynasty who ruled at Golconda from 1580-1611 and founded the present city of Hyderabad, was himself a considerable poet in Urdu. The style of Urdu, as developed in the Deccan with its inevitable mixture of words of southern Prakrits, came to

* It was also 'mixed' in another sense. Amir Khusrau started the fashion of composing ghazals with alternate lines in Persian and Hindi.

be known as Dakhani. With the migration in the 18th century of the most important Dakhani poet Wali to Delhi, the major centre of development shifted to the Moghul capital. Delhi later shared this honour with Lucknow.

Urdu, indeed, was the only major Indian language to prosper in the 18th century which was in general the dark age of Indian literature. The famous 'Four Pillars of Urdu', Wali, Mir, Sauda and Dard, belong to the 18th century. But every privilege has its price, and Urdu was to suffer the fate of all pampered children of wealthy parents. It luxuriated in its solitary affluence, drawing more embellishment than nourishment from imported influences and becoming increasingly subjective, sophisticated and morbid with the decline of the power of its ruling patrons.* Nor is it without a certain significance that its greatest poet Ghalib with whom the modern age of Urdu is said to begin was still composing doleful—though exquisite—ghazals redolent of Persian aroma, when Bankim, Madhusudan and Dinabandhu were cutting out new paths for Indian literature. Instead of marching ahead to conquer fresh fields, the gift-

---

* A story related of Mir, the foremost ghazal poet of Urdu, is significant. His patron, the Nawab of Lucknow, gave him a room to live which overlooked a beautiful garden. The window which opened on to the garden was, however, always kept closed by the poet. When asked why, he replied, 'I am always engaged in tending the flowers of my fancy. What need or time have I for these ordinary flowers?'

ed poets of Urdu were singing dirges on the ruins of a feudal glory or indulging in clever sophistications.* It was in the hands of Ghalib's successors, Hali and Iqbal, and mainly in, or on the eve of, the 20th century that Urdu woke up to its new destiny.

To some extent, Kashmiri, Punjabi and Sindhi, which shared with Urdu the legacy of Persian and used its script or a modified form of it, had had also a rich flowering in the 18th century—the lyrics and ballads of Bullhe Shah and Waris Shah in Punjabi, of Shah Latif in Sindhi and the exquisite songs of Arnimal, the deserted tragic wife of a Brahmin, in Kashmiri. But these three languages were overshadowed by the cultural glamour of Urdu and their modern development was unduly retarded. All the more credit to the pioneers who

---

* Ghalib who died in 1869 may be said to mark the many-splendoured sunset of a great era rather than the beginning of a new age. Original, subtle and daring in thought he was a more gifted poet than most of his contemporaries in his own or other Indian languages, and might have led the modern age if the circumstances had been more fortunate for him. A court-poet of Delhi he was a witness to the tragic collapse of the Moghul Empire after the 1857 uprising, and could hardly be expected to feel any enthusiasm for the culture of the upstart foreigners from across the seas. As he himself put it: 'I have been a helpless witness of man killing man; I have watched an Emperor taken captive and exiled to an alien land; I have felt old foundations shifting as on sand and crashing. So have I lived and passed my days. How can I bring myself to say that God exists, God the Bounteous Giver, God the Beneficent?'—Kaul, J. L., *Interpretations of Ghalib*, Atma Ram and Sons, Delhi, 1957.

bravely held aloft the banner of their mother tongue when it hardly paid to do so—Mahjoor and Master Zinda Kaul in Kashmiri, Pooran Singh and Vir Singh in Punjabi, and Kalich Beg and Kauromal in Sindhi.

What might surprise one is the tardy and somewhat faltering advent of the modern upsurge in the Dravidian languages which had had a longer and richer literary tradition than the northern Indo-Aryan speeches as well as an earlier and closer contact with the Christian missions. The past, it would seem, has weighed more heavily on the south than on the north in India, and on none more heavily than on Tamil which of all the living languages of modern India can claim the most venerable ancestry. However, in course of time the impulse of the age broke through the crust and these languages too responded to it creatively, in a flowering increasingly abundant. Among the stalwarts who led the way were Bharati and Kalki in Tamil, Puttana and Srikantia in Kannada, Viresalingam and Guruzada Apparao in Telugu, with Kerala Varma and Chandu Menon in Malayalam. It is worth noting that the youngest of these Dravidian languages, Malayalam, has responded to the new age more vigorously than the oldest, Tamil, which even now looks too wistfully to the past. What Tagore called 'the old man's ghost' sits on the shoulders of all of us, but on some it presses more heavily than on others.

Thus the basic trend in the development of modern age in Indian literature, whose early course has been outlined above, was conditioned by the response of a newly oriented intelligentsia to the freshly discovered patterns of Western thought and expression as revealed through English education. Its first achievement was to fashion the much-needed instruments of the new expression, and to discover in prose a vital medium of thought-communication for the modern age. Several new literary modes were also assimilated in the native media, like the blank verse, sonnet, novel, short story, essay, etc. But more important than the form or shape of the container is what is poured into it. Not the finest decanter is of any use if the contents lack the fire of spirit. It was the exuberance of spirit bubbling over in response to the challenge from the West which was the real maker of modern Indian literature.

So exhilarating was this spirit that it did not seem to matter if the contents were served in bottles old-fashioned and borrowed. Indeed, some of the Western forms had already lost their vogue in their land of origin when they were adopted in Indian languages, e.g., Walter Scott's historical romances on which Bankim's novels were modelled. Nevertheless, what Bankim did was both original and revolutionary in the context of the state of letters in Bengal at that time. 'Bankim Chandra was brave enough to go against the orthodoxy which believed in the security of tombstones and in that finality which can only belong to the lifeless.' * In other words what Bankim did was to pour such new life that what was elsewhere an old and worn-out form glowed with a new vitality in the Indian context.

This was even more true of Madhusudan's epics. Bankim, at any rate, has had many imitators and followers, but Madhusudan hardly any, if for no other reason than that the epic is not suited to the modern temper and need. Nevertheless, if Madhusudan eminently succeeded in his mission, it was because he gave expression to the new exuberance of spirit in a way which was almost like the churning of an ocean. He discovered and showed what Bengali language was capable of. Both by temperament and talent Rabindranath Tagore was utterly unlike his predecessor, and may even be said to be antipathic, and yet he paid him this glowing tribute : 'The most daring feat was by Michael Madhusudan, the first pioneer in modern Bengali poetry. Nothing could be stranger or more unfamiliar to the Bengali reader than the appearance

---

* Tagore, Rabindranath, *The Religion of an Artist.*

of that flood of high-sounding difficult words *à la* Milton, with which Michael made the Bengali language undulate with waves of words. . . . Thanks to the extraordinary genius of Madhusudan the East and the West met for the first time in Bengali poetry.' *

This early overflow of exuberance was naturally romantic in feeling and tone. The first flush of discovery, of one's own potential as well as of the opportunities available, is always exciting. Endless vistas seem to open before the mind's eye and there is no limit to man's faith in his power and destiny. Says Iqbal in one of his Persian poems :

> Thou didst create night and I made the lamp.
> Thou didst create clay and I made the cup.
> Thou didst create the deserts, mountains and
> > forests,
> I produced the orchards, gardens and the groves;
> It is I who makes glass out of stone,
> And it is I who turns a poison into
> an antidote †

Linked to this aspect of wide-eyed romanticism is the other aspect that comes from intoxication with one's ego, the mistaken assumption, in the

* 'Adhunik Bangla Kabita', Rabindranath Tagore, *Kabi O Kabita*, Vol. I, No. 1, Calcutta. English translation (of the passage quoted) by Dr Lokenath Bhattacharya.

† Quoted in *Iqbal: His Art and Thought* by Syed Abdul Vahid, Lahore, 1944.

first flush of excitement, that the ego and personality are identical. The excitement is all the greater in the case of a people disciplined for centuries in the rigid moulds of scriptural and social conformism. Tagore has related in his *Reminiscences* how the sudden revelation of the self's validity, that I am what I am, had affected him and his contemporaries in early youth, and has quoted a popular verse of that period :

> My heart is mine,
> I have sold it to none,
> Be it tattered and torn and worn away,
> My heart is mine!

One is reminded of the much more famous lines of the Urdu poet Ghalib:

> It's a heart—not a piece of brick or stone—
> Why should it not fill with pain?
> Yes, I shall weep and wail—a thousand times,
> Why need others molest me for it.

Iqbal goes even further : *

> Even if one iota is to be diminished from my
> being,
> I shall not accept life immortal at this price.

And again :

> The pangs of yearning constitute a priceless
> commodity,

* *Ibid.*

I shall not exchange my humanity even for
divinity.

The high-pitched exuberance natural to this stage of self-discovery was reinforced by the influence of the romantic phase through which Western literature itself was passing, or had recently passed. The impact of Western thought had, however, another far-reaching consequence not directly related to literature. The emphasis on democracy and self-expression in English, French and American writing and institutions could not but stimulate in the Indian intelligentsia a patriotic and nationalist consciousness with its search for roots of self-respect, a pride in one's ancestral heritage and an inevitable resentment of foreign imposition. Tagore's novel *Gora* is a masterly analysis of this built-in conflict in the very nature of this cultural resurgence, a conflict which still persists and colours not only our literature but almost every aspect of life. The result was a certain dichotomy in the mental and moral attitude of the writers, some welcoming the new movement, some resenting it.

So deep-rooted was and is this dichotomy that the same writer may look wistfully backward with one eye, and longingly ahead with the other. Sri Aurobindo's exaltation of the Indian cultural values is well known, * though he was educated in the West, in an English public school and uni-

* See *The Foundations of Indian Culture*, Sri Aurobindo Library Inc, New York, 1953.

versity, and could hardly speak his mother tongue when he returned to his land. There has always been in all countries and times a conflict between the old and the new, but in India, because the new was identified with an alien culture and foreign domination, the clash of loyalties has been sharper. The case of Bankim Chandra, a leading herald of the new, who looked more and more wistfully to the past as he grew older, has already been cited. Tilak in Marathi and Bharati in Tamil were even more extravagant in their native pride and have their counterparts in all Indian languages. Bharati's poetry overflowed with such adulation :

> The mighty Himavant is ours—
> There is no equal anywhere on earth;
> The generous Ganga is ours—
> Which other river can match her grace?

> The sacred Upanishads are ours—
> What scriptures else to name with them?
> This sunny golden land is ours—
> She's peerless, let us praise her! *

He also wrote an ecstatic ode to Tilak oozing sentiments as the following :

> He is the love-fed honey-dripping
> Bud of our Renaissance;
> He is the symbol and security

* Prema, S., *Bharati in English Verse*, Madras, 1958.

Of our reviving nationhood. *

Fanned by political aspirations, this pride in India's past grew more inflamed, and provided increasing fuel to the passion for national freedom. While thus serving a useful historical purpose, it was not without its unhealthy aspect insofar as it encouraged an exaggerated self-righteousness and distorted the correct historical perspective. Even so chaste and universal a spirit as Mahatma Gandhi could for a while fall under its spell and utter with passionate sincerity the dismal half-truth that British association had ruined India not only economically but intellectually, morally and spiritually.† Such a reaction was, however, inevitable

* *Ibid.*

† Tagore's attitude, on the other hand, was very different. He attributed the robustness of India's spiritual thought to its capacity to assimilate alien influences. This was repeatedly stressed by him. His famous poem, 'Bharat-tirtha', first published in *Gitanjali* (original Bengali edition), 1910, is an invocation to this spirit of India, and ends on this note:

> Come ye Aryan, come non-Aryan, Hindu, Muslim,
> come,
> Come ye English, come ye Christian, welcome
> everyone,
> Come Brahmin, cleanse your mind and clasp the hand
> of all,
> Come ye outcaste, come ye lowly, fling away the load
> of shame,
> Come, one and all, ...
> To the shore of this vast sea of humanity
> That is India.

under the circumstances, and was itself a lesson learnt from the virulent development of nationalism in the West.

A romantic faith in the future of man, a sudden awareness of the wonderland of nature and life, an aggressive consciousness of one's individuality, and an increasingly articulate assertion of one's full rights as a human being—all these were various aspects of the general impact of Western humanism. Humanism as such was nothing new. The long tradition of unfettered speculation on the mystery of life and universe and the concept of *moksha* or liberation as the goal of spiritual striving, from the time of the Buddha and the Upanishads to the medieval Vaishnav and Sufi poetry, bear ample witness to it. What was, however, new was the secular emphasis of humanism, its detachment from religion and unconcern with spiritual values as such.

And so Indian literature, almost from the beginning of its modern phase, was gradually and steadily coloured by political aspirations passionately voiced in almost every language of the country. The spiritual note of Indian poetic tradition which had attained a rapturous and poignant pitch in the medieval outpourings of saint-poets and mystics became fainter and fainter until it was drowned by the clamour of earthly pains and longings. Tagore's *Gitanjali* is the swan song of this great tradition.* The devotional content of poetry has been increasingly replaced by the political, the ethical bias by the ideological, the plaintive tone by strident challenge, until the dominant note of contemporary Indian writing is that of protest and mockery.

Tagore's influence, after the award of the Nobel Prize in 1913, crossed the frontiers of Bengal and

---

* Religious poetry continues to be written to this day and in a fairly abundant measure, but in the main it is little better than an inane repetition of what had been expressed very much better earlier.

was for some time a source of exhilaration, if not always of inspiration, to his contemporaries all over India, from Master Zinda Kaul in Kashmir to Kumaran Asan in Kerala. There is hardly an outstanding pioneer of modern poetry in any language of India, except perhaps Urdu, who escaped this impact. The literary influence proper was, however, not deep, since most of his non-Bengali admirers knew his work only through English translation. The influence was more fruitful in the case of languages where the young poets took the trouble to read him at first hand. The Chhayavad or Romantic movement in Hindi poetry, led by 'Nirala', Pant and others, which has served as a potent stimulus in the development of modern Hindi literature, was largely inspired by it. On the whole, the main impact of Tagore outside Bengal was indirect. He gave confidence to Indian writers and stimulated their faith in their own language and lore. What could be done in one Indian language could be done in any other. This creative confidence with which he inspired writers to write in their own languages, to draw their sustenance from their own roots, was Tagore's greatest service to Indian literature. Not always obvious, but nonetheless real.

More obvious, and indeed glaringly so since 1920, was the impact of Gandhi, Marx and Freud. An odd trinity. None of them was a man of letters proper. Each was in his own way a prophet with a rod of authority which shook the mind more vigorously than any literary charm could do.

They conditioned mental attitudes, provoked intellectual turmoil and released moral passions which had effects, profound and widespread. Gandhi's impact, due mainly to the magnetism of his personality and the special circumstances in India, was confined to writers in his own country. That of the other two was more intellectual and abstract, and therefore universal. Indian writers felt it, not directly so much as through writers elsewhere.

Gandhi's impact on Indian writers was direct and widespread. Apart from its political repercussions, it was both moral and intellectual and at once inhibitive and liberating. Insofar as it sharpened the writer's loyalties by narrowing them and encouraged puritanism and a horror of sex, it was inhibitive and unhealthy and resulted, without meaning to, in an irritating sanctimoniousness. But by and large it was a liberating force and not only widened the range of the writer's sympathy but also heightened its intensity. Gandhi stripped urban life and 'elegance' of their pretensions and emphasised that religion without compassion and culture without conscience were worthless. He transfigured the image of India and turned national idealism from its futile adulation of the past to face the reality of India as she was—poor, starving and helpless, but with an untapped potential of unlimited possibilities.

Both Vivekananda and Tagore had said the same thing earlier, but it was Gandhi more than any one else who made this image vivid and poignantly real and succeeded in imparting a new insight to the Indian intelligentsia, enlarging their sympathies and adding a new dimension to their aspirations. Indian writers learnt to see their country, not in the splendid ruins of ancient monuments, not in the temples of Banaras and Madurai, not in the stately mansions overlooking the Malabar Hill and Chowringhee, but in the teeming slums of Bombay and Calcutta, and in the innumerable villages of India sunk in poverty and squalor, the stinking 'dung hills', as Gandhi called them. He thus provided a powerful ethical stimulus to the literary trend, which had already begun, from romanticism to realism, from self-adulation to self-analysis.

Gandhi also hastened the transition from the highflown, artificial, 'literary' style to the vogue of the spoken form. His own employment of a simple and direct style, compact and incisive, shorn of all superfluities, both in English and his mother tongue Gujarati, was a very healthy corrective to the natural tendency to flambuoyance in Indian writing. This influence was particularly fruitful in Gujarati which language he himself wielded with masterly ease and economy. In Bengali the crispness of the colloquial speech had already achieved a literary status in the writings of Tagore and his young friend, Pramatha Chaudhury, who wrote under the pen-name of 'Birbal' and who introduced into Bengali some of the precision and sophisticated charm which he had imbibed from his love of French language and literature.

The eminent Hindi novelist Premchand has described in an autobiographical essay how, inspired by the Mahatma, he resigned from Government service and settled down in a village to see life in the raw and to write about it. His later career as the foremost novelist in Hindi (as also in Urdu), his insight into the life of the village folk, his abounding sympathy with their unhappy, stunted lives, and his simple and direct delineation of it was a major influence on many of his contemporaries, and reflects the impact of Gandhi on modern literature in India. Among other writers of note who responded to this impact, each in his fashion, may be mentioned the gifted Gupta brothers, Maithilisharan and Siyaramsharan, as well as Jainendra Kumar, in Hindi, Kaka Kalelkar, 'Darshak' and Umashankar Joshi in Gujarati, Sane Guruji, Khandekar and Mama Warerkar in Marathi, Nilmani Phookan in Assamese, Kalindi Charan Panigrahi in Oriya, Annadashankar Ray in Bengali, Bharati in Tamil, Vallathol in Malayalam, and many more in these and other languages.

Paradoxical as it may sound, the dynamics of Gandhian thought helped to open the way for the influx of Marxism in the literary field in India. Perhaps there is no paradox. The basic attraction of both the Gandhian and Marxian appeals—at any rate to the Indian intelligentsia—was their idealism, however much the ideological framework and the terminology employed differed. Gandhi's lifelong crusade against colonial exploitation of the weaker nations by the stronger, his no less vehement condemnation of any form of economic exploitation, his insistence that what is not shared with the dispossessed is stolen from them, and his passionate confession that he was ashamed to talk of God to a people whose stomachs were crying for bread—these rather than his exaltation of prayer and fast, of spinning and celibacy, of non-violence in thought, word and deed, had impressed the Indian intelligentsia. Between this aspect of Gandhian crusade and the almost parallel faith of Marxism the major difference that struck the Indian intellectual was that the Marxian dogma appeared to be more consistent in its ideology and more realistic in its interpretation of history. This explains the phenomenon of the 'thirties when many writers and intellectuals who were first inspired by Gandhi later veered towards socialist or Marxist ideologies. Premchand who began as an ardent admirer of Gandhi presided over the first session of the communist-sponsored Progressive Writers Association in 1936, and came to believe more and more in the desperate remedies advocated by Marxism.*

The eruption of Marxism on the Indian literary scene in the early 'thirties is a phenomenon which India shared with many other countries. To Gandhi is due the credit that its manifestation on the

---

* See his wife's reminiscences: *Prem Chand Ghar Main* (Premchand at Home) by Shivrani Devi. See also 'Rabhar' Hans Raj, *Prem Chand: His Life and Work*, Atma Ram & Sons, Delhi, 1957.

Indian soil was neither virulent nor on the whole unhealthy. The popular imagination had already been oriented by him to look for God, not in the temple, mosque or church, but in *daridra-narayana,* the divine in the image of the hungry outcaste. This had given an ethical glamour to leftist sensibility so that to be radical was to be almost virtuous. On the other hand, class-hatred was softened and rendered comparatively innocuous. A Vallathol could see no contradiction in invoking both Lenin and Mary Magdalene with equal lyrical fervour. Premchand who came to be called the Gorky of India ended his autobiographical testament with a characteristic Vaishnav affirmation that not a blade of grass stirs but as God wills it. And so, too, many novelists with professed Marxist allegiance are not ashamed in India to reveal their sympathy with what would be condemned as purely bourgeois sensibilities by orthodox Marxists.

Influence of the Freudian interpretation of human behaviour has been more subtle, though less overwhelming, than that of dialectic materialism. In a sense more widespread, too, its appeal being more universal and its analysis independent of class affiliation or ideology. Indian writers, in particular poets and novelists, have come increasingly under its spell, despite Gandhi to whom sex was sin except in the service of legitimate procreation. The ancient and once traditional Hindu outlook on sex was healthy, amoral and unashamed. The hymns of the *Rig Veda* are interspersed with verses which glow with the primal passion.* If Vatsyayana's *Kama-sutra* has today provoked among readers in India and abroad an unhealthy interest bordering on the pornographic, it is a reflection of the morbid state of the contemporary consciousness and not of any perversity or moral degeneracy in the outlook of its author or of the age in which such works were taken seriously as learned treatises or shastras.

The medieval devotional poetry of Vidyapati, Surdas and many others could revel in a voluptuous and not unoften frankly erotic symbolism which the orthodox scholarship would fain slur over. Such erotic expression was obviously not inconsistent with flights of spiritual ecstasy or moral piety. But the influence of Victorian squeamishness and of its counterpart in the Brahmo reformism of Bengal, reinforced by the puritan crusade of Gandhi, had overlaid the Indian consciousness with a layer of inhibitions so thick that it needed the prestige of a scientific dogma to break through. How partial and fumbling was this break-through is best illustrated in the case of Premchand and a large number of writers even

* As in the dialogue of Yama and Yami, the primeval twins, where the sister passionately wooes the brother:

> I, Yami, am possessed by love of Yama,
> That I may rest on the same couch beside him.
> I as a wife would yield me to my husband,
> Like car-wheels let us speed in the same task.

—See De, S. K., *Ancient Indian Erotics and Erotic Literature*, Firma K. L. Mukhopadhyaya, Calcutta, 1959.

today who are 'progressive' politically and look upon Freud as the corrupter of morals.*

To these two foreign and non-literary influences, namely, Marxian dialectics and Freudian probings, may be added a literary one proper, also imported from the West. This relates to the new experiments in form known under various high-sounding names which have achieved increasing prestige in the West and are associated with the names of Marcel Proust, James Joyce, Ezra Pound, T. S. Eliot, Jean Paul Sartre, Camus, and many others. Being innovations or deviations mainly in form and technique, they are independent of any particular faith or political ideology. A writer may be very daring and original in expression, but conservative in religious or political faith, or vice versa. T. S. Eliot was a curious illustration of this amalgam of originality and conformism. Among Indian writers,

* 'The only benefit Padma derived from education,' says Premchand ironically in a short story, 'was that she thought sexual satisfaction to be the end of life. Any restriction was poison to soul. Freud was her deity and the principal guide to her life.' Quoted in *Prem Chand: His Life and Work* by Hans Raj 'Rahbar'. The author also quotes Premchand's conversation with Jainendra Kumar, a leading Hindi novelist, in which Premchand complained that Bengali literature was preoccupied with sex. 'The Bengalis,' he added, 'are a reflective and sentimental people. Reflection and sentimentality reach to places which I can never dream of attaining. My logic and realism are limited; but I believe in restraint and a very firm purpose. Rabindranath and Sarat Chandra are great indeed, but I doubt if Hindi writers ought to follow them. At least, I won't.'

Bishnu Dey and Buddhadev Bose in Bengali, 'Ajneya' and Muktibodh in Hindi, Mardhekar and Vinda Karandikar in Marathi and a host of other parallels in these and other languages of the country share a common iconoclastic zeal in form but are loyal to their respective orthodoxies, political or any other.

These influences did not work singly or in isolation, but in a mixed and jumbled fashion as most things do in life. A poet may be very modern and daring and yet steer clear of any sex obsession, like Jibanananda Das,* sensuous, earthy, with almost a savage delight in touch and smell, but robustly free from any sexual gloating; or Amiya Chakravarty, a globe-trotter and voluntary exile from his land, a modern among moderns who has not learnt to mistake loudness for virility. A writer may be a profound Gandhian and swear by non-violence and yet be obsessed with sex in his novels, like the talented Hindi writer, Jainendra Kumar. The impact, on the whole, of these various influences in their mixed interaction has been salutary and stimulating, despite a wild aberration here and there. The orthodox smugness, with its sentimental piety and adulation of the past, needed a rough jolt which they provided.

* For English rendering of nine poems of his see *The Beloit Poetry Journal*, Fall, 1965.

A major characteristic of the modern age, in India as in the West, and more so perhaps in the United States than elsewhere, is the quick turn-over of everything, goods and machines as well as ideas and influences. Nothing retains its vogue for long. Although Tagore's place in Bengali is unchallenged and will be so for a long time to come, his influence on his contemporaries, once dominant, came to be increasingly questioned and defied from about the 'twenties onwards. Tagore himself had led the earlier revolt against orthodoxy and had long blasted what he had picturesquely caricatured as the castle of conformism in his drama *Achalayatan.* But the adulation of Tagore was itself becoming an orthodoxy which provoked a group of young and gifted writers who came to be known as the Kallol group to proclaim their revolt. *Kallol,* which began as a modest four-anna story-magazine, soon gathered round it a galaxy of young talent, Nazrul Islam, Jibanananda Das, Buddhadeva Bose, Premendra Mitra, and many others, most of them established celebrities now.

The revolt yielded a rich harvest, although it was not long before it was discovered that Tagore himself was no less audacious, and could, when he chose, outmodern most moderns.*

The most dynamic creative force in the cultural resurgence of modern India as indeed its finest achievement, it was nevertheless inevitable that Indian literature in its later contemporary phase should outgrow Tagore's influence and even to some extent repudiate it. He himself was well aware of it, and not merely anticipated it but showed the way. In a mood, half playful, half earnest, he framed a formidable diatribe against himself and put it in the mouth of his chief character in his novel *Sesher Kavita,* published in 1929: 'The strongest objection against Rabindranath Tagore is that this gentleman, imitating old Wordsworth, insists most perversely on continuing. Many a time the messenger of Death has called to switch off the light, but even as the old man rises from his throne, he still clings to its arms. If he doesn't quit

---

* Bose, Buddhadeva, *An Acre of Green Grass*, Orient Longmans, Calcutta, 1948. The following comment of the talented author, himself a leader of this group, is worth citing: 'I do not know that any single poet in history so completely permeated the language and the literature of his country and his time as Rabindranath in his later years. Inevitably and rightly, young poets were steeped in him; but what was neither inevitable nor right was that many, instead of journeying with him and in him, were led to use his as an anchor. For these, it was impossible not to imitate Rabindranath, and it was impossible to imitate Rabindranath.'

of his own accord, it becomes our duty to quit his court in a body. The one who succeeds him will also enter in triumph, thundering and bragging that there shall be no end to his rule, that the very heavens shall be chained to the gate of his mortal abode. For a time his devotees will feed him and fête him and adore him, until the auspicious hour of the sacrifice arrives, when the devotees will clamour for liberation from the bondage of devotion. Such is the way the four-footed god is worshipped in Africa. Such is also the way the two-footed, three-footed, four-footed and fourteen-footed gods of metre may be worshipped. No desecration can compare with the profanity of dragging out devotion till it is hackneyed.'

This cyclic phenomenon of idol-breakers themselves being installed as idols, and younger iconoclasts swinging their axes at them, has been paralleled in almost all Indian languages and has been on the whole a healthy, lively and fruitful trend, both in poetry and prose. While doughty champions of the orthodox sentiment and form continue to hold their own (it is doubtful if they will ever disappear unless India ceases to be India), like Visvanadha Satyanarayana in Telugu, S. V. Ranganna in Kannada, Mahadevi Varma in Hindi, and many more in Urdu and other languages, it is the spirit of non-conformism and experiment that gives variety, colour and pep to much of modern writing in India.*

* It might, however, be pointed out that certain qualities of form and mood which are considered modern and

Although poetry continues to be popular in India and its public recitation at a symposium, known as *mushaira* in Urdu and *kavi-sammelan* in Hindi, is always an event of considerable popular interest and may attract an audience of several thousand, poetry hardly suits the temper of the modern society, increasingly industrial and mechanised. If poetry continues to be written in India in such profusion and declaimed with such exuberance or gusto, it is partly because the tradition of verse chanted or sung is very old and deep-rooted, and partly because a certain prestige attaches to poetry as 'purer' literature than any other, and in India a certain holiness, too, the earlier *kavis* being venerated as seers and saints. Even so, poetry in its narrative form as epic and ballad has lost its ancient vogue and has yielded its place to the novel and the short story which are today the

have been consciously derived from the West need not have been so derived if our poets were more familiar with the indigenous variety. The prose poem, for example, was a familiar form in Kannada *vachanas* many centuries before it gained a vogue in the USA and Europe. Take the following Gond (a so-called savage tribe) song quoted by Verrier Elwin:

> As they plough the fields
> the she-cobra hisses.
> O my darling, you are my life ...
> But as the cobra hisses
> So will I
> if you are faithless.

A modern poet might have 'hissed' likewise.

most widely and best cultivated form of literature, with a contemporary output both voluminous and lively.

Both these forms, as stated earlier, received their first stimulus in Bengal and attained maturity with Bankim and Tagore. Since then they have achieved phenomenal vogue in the hands of their successors, among whom Sarat Chandra Chatterji won a popularity, both in and outside Bengal, which for a time surpassed that of Tagore's. A keen observer of the middle-class domestic scene and a master of tenderness and pathos, Sarat Chandra's genuine sympathy for the socially unfortunate, his idyllic portraiture of 'noble' prostitutes and 'innocent' rakes, combined with a sneaking regard for Hindu sentiment, made him an idol of adolescent males and of women of all ages. He was perhaps the first writer of modern India to amass a not negligible fortune solely from his royalties.

Very different from Sarat Chandra but no less remarkable in his own way was Bibhuti Bhushan Banerji. Though he failed to achieve Sarat Chandra's spectacular success in his lifetime, his novel *Pather Panchali* is today more widely known than perhaps any other Indian novel. It is a rustic idyll, a wayside ballad, as its name implies, a narration of great simplicity and charm, utterly free from any affectation. Long before Satyajit Ray's exquisite screen version of the story made the novel internationally known, Rabindranath Tagore had hailed it with warm appreciation. 'No attempt is made,' he wrote in the Bengali journal *Parichaya*

(Baisakh, 1340), 'to beguile the reader's mind with high sentiments wrapped in cheap tinsel. The book stands on its own merit. I felt in it the true flavour of story-telling. It does not set out to teach anything, it helps one to see things—trees and shrubs, highways and byways, men and women, their joys and woes—in a wholly new and fresh light, cleansed of their humdrum triviality.'

Tarashankar Banerji, Manik Bandyopadhyay, Premendra Mitra, Sailajananda Mukhopadhyay, Annadasankar Ray, 'Bonophul', Subodh Ghosh and a host of other novelists and short story writers in Bengali have maintained a fairly high standard and have handled the art of fiction with originality and skill. They are matched by notable contemporaries in other languages of the country—Jainendra Kumar and Yashpal in Hindi, Thakazhi (whose *Chemmeen* has been published in English and many other foreign languages) and Basheer in Malayalam, the Mohanty brothers in Oriya, Biren Bhattacharya and Abdul Malik in Assamese, Masti and Karanth in Kannada, Khandekar and Gadgil in Marathi, Pannalal Patel and 'Darshak' in Gujarati, Mi Pa Somasundaram and Akilan in Tamil, Bapiraju and Gopichand in Telugu, Nanak Singh and Duggal in Punjabi, Krishan Chunder and Bedi in Urdu, and many more in these and other languages.*

---

* These names are illustrative and would have many parallels. See *Contemporary Indian Literature* (Sahitya Akademi, New Delhi, 2nd ed., 1959) as well as annual surveys of contemporary literary output in Indian languages

A few general observations may be hazarded. Several fiction writers in India are also poets of considerable merit; in some cases, perhaps better poets than novelists, like 'Ajneya'* in Hindi, Buddhadeva Bose in Bengali, Somasundaram in Tamil, and Amrita Pritam in Punjabi. Most of them have written both novels and short stories, and are generally more skilled and effective as short story writers than as novelists. They cover a wide range of theme, and vary in scope, mood and technical treatment. Some of them, like Tarashankar in Bengali and 'Renu' in Hindi, have caught the accent and idiosyncracy of a particular region in their novels, in the manner, if not in the tragic intensity, of Thomas Hardy; some like 'Ajneya' in Hindi, or Manik Bandyopadhyay in Bengali, probe the dark caverns of the human mind, although no Dostoevsky is yet born in India; some like Thakazhi in Malayalam, Abdul Malik in Assamese, Yashpal in Hindi, Kishan Chunder in Urdu have an ideological bias and write with a mission; some, like Sailajananda, are content to reveal with grim objectivity the dark and ugly areas of social injustice; some, like the inimitable 'Parshuram', † expose the shams of society with a kindly eye, though a Dickens is yet to arrive. The historical novel, ever since Bankim Chandra gave

published in the Sahitya Akademi's journal, *Indian Literature*.

  * Pen-name of S. H. Vatsyayan.

  † Pen-name of the versatile Bengali author, Rajsekhara Bose.

it vogue, has had considerable popularity, and ambitious volumes have been published recreating (with more embellishment than art) 'heroic' incidents from Indian history.

But whether the treatment is romantic, realistic or impressionist, whether the exploration is historical, regional, tribal, social or psychological, the bias Gandhian, Marxian or Freudian, the mood hilarious or grim, the writers have by and large continued the tradition of humanism and of sympathy for the fallen bequeathed by Tagore, Sarat Chandra and Premchand. Except for a few aberrations, they have not yet succumbed to the morbid spell of cynicism, violence and sex-obsession which is become the bane of their highbrow counterparts in some countries of the West. Most of them still tell a story that entertains the reader (whatever else it may do by way of provoking, prodding or persuading him) which is what fiction is primarily intended to do.

It might also be added that these writers represent not only a medley of techniques and styles but also uneven levels of creative achievement. From *Srikanta* of Sarat Chandra or *Pather Panchali* of Bibhuti Bhushan or *Jhootha Sach* of Yashpal to a plethora of so-called modern classics with their plots borrowed from Scott or Dickens, Hugo or Balzac, D. H. Lawrence or Hemingway (even *East Lynne* of Mrs Henry Wood has been reborn as an Indian classic) is a far cry. But India is a land of contrasts.

The number of women writers of fiction is not negligible. The tradition of Tagore's elder sister, Swarnakumari Devi, who was the first accomplished literary woman to write original novels in modern India, has been maintained by many contemporary writers of distinction, among them Ashapurna Devi and Protibha Bose in Bengali, Basanta Kumari in Oriya, Ismet Chugtai and Qurratulain Hyder in Urdu, Usha Priyamvada in Hindi, Malati Bedekar in Marathi, Amrita Pritam in Punjabi and many others. Fortunately, there is no social prejudice against women adopting literary careers, and no need to masquerade as a George Eliot or a George Sand.*

* On the other hand, a leading writer and poet of Assam, the late Dr Birinchi Kumar Barua, published his famous novel, *Seuji Patar Kahini,* depicting the life of tea-plantation labour, under the feminine pen-name of Bina Barua.

Among Indian languages Sanskrit occupies a unique place. The parent of most Indian languages and source of inspiration and strength to all of them, it has held its own through many vicissitudes over a period of more than 3,000 years during which many Prakrits and Apabhramsas born of its womb grew up, flourished and perished. No doubt, in a simpler and less sophisticated form it was once a spoken tongue, but in course of time it acquired a form so rigidly classical that it ceased to be the speech of the people and became an almost exclusive preserve of pundits and priests. Paradoxically, it is by dying as a living speech that Sanskrit has survived and weathered the storms of centuries. It has therefore been sometimes called a 'dead' language—dead only in the sense that it is not the everyday speech of any compact mass of people. Otherwise it continues to be, as it has always been, not only a very vital source on which almost all other Indian languages, except High Urdu and, perhaps, modern Tamil in its recent phase,* draw for their vocabulary, but also a living fount of literary inspiration to Indian writers. Save in the case of Urdu, there are hardly any writers of outstanding distinction in the modern period who have not drawn freely on the wealth of both Sanskrit and Western literatures, though some have taken more from the one than from the other. The poetry of Sudhindranath Datta, a leading modern poet of Bengal whose premature death in 1961 was a grievous loss to Bengali letters, was as remarkable for the effects created by its use of Sanskrit diction as for the influence it reflected of Eliot, Baudelaire and other Western writers.† The curious blend of Sanskrit and the ultra-modern West or, as in the case of the prolific Hindi writer Rahul Sankrityayan, of Sanskrit and Marx, is not an uncommon feature of contemporary Indian writing.

However, quite apart from the unrivalled posi-

* 'In the latest Tamil literature, as in Tamil society,' write the learned authors of *A History of Tamil Literature* (Y.M.C.A. Publishing House, Calcutta, 1961), 'the strongest trends fall under two sharp divisions, pro-Brahminist and anti-Brahminist.' Sanskrit, being identified with the former, is so taboo to the latter that a distinguished writer discarded his name, Swami Vedachalam, as Sanskrit-derived, and adopted the purely Dravidian-sounding Maraimalai Adihal. He 'even claims the Upanishads as Dravidian thought'.

† His first major book of poems was published under the title, *Orchestra*. Another and no less distinguished contemporary, Bishnu Dey, has entitled one of his books of poetry, *Urvasi O Artemis*.

tion of Sanskrit as the main treasure-house of Indian thought, religion and literary achievement, and its significant role in the development of medieval as well as modern Indian literature, Sanskrit continues to be used even today as a literary vehicle for scholarly and speculative as well as literary writing, overriding all linguistic boundaries in India. It is the only language in which indigenous learning has maintained an unbroken tradition of more than three thousand years and in which scholars from Kashmir to Kerala, from Punjab to Assam, meet on a truly common platform, irrespective of their regional tongues and independent of any Western aid.

It is also a remarkable fact that neither its prestige nor is popularity was adversely affected in the long run by the spread of English education in the country. In fact, the contribution of Western scholars and indologists has not only made available to Indian readers many hidden treasures of Sanskrit not easily accessible before and enabled them to appreciate its vast and varied heritage better, but has also encouraged its study in schools and colleges in a modern and scientific manner. What was once the exclusive preserve of a privileged caste is today become the common heritage of all. Sanskrit and English are in no sense rivals in India, and some of the best Indian writing interpretative of Sanskrit philosophy is in English language.*

* The works of Dr S. Radhakrishnan and of Sri Aurobindo provide in themselves a monumental testimony, not

In an odd sense English shares with Sanskrit a twofold national role—as being equally accessible to all irrespective of regional and linguistic affiliations, and as providing a common source from which the modern Indian languages have drawn both stimulus and sustenance. Odd, because in another sense, no two languages are more antithetical, inasmuch as no language is so national as Sanskrit and none so unnational as English in India.

Those who make a virtue of patriotism resent the current use of English in India as a relic of erstwhile foreign domination. On the other hand, English is still the major medium of higher education in most Indian universities, specially in science, medicine and technology which are the backbone of modern education, as also the major means of communication among the intelligentsia all over India. Whatever the patriotic sentiment, the curious fact that it was the only language in which Gandhiji could communicate with Tagore or with Rajagopalachari and in which Nehru as the Prime Minister of India could discuss matters of state with the then President Dr Radhakrishnan, as also the fact that the Collected Works of Mahatma Gandhi are being edited and published (under the direct auspices of the Government of

to mention a large number of other scholars. For an excellent survey of contemporary writing in Sanskrit, the reader may refer to Dr V. Raghavan's chapter on 'Sanskrit Literature' in *Contemporary Indian Literature*, published by Sahitya Akademi, New Delhi, 2nd ed., 1959.

India) in English, is each a commentary by itself on the current usefulness of this language in India, at any rate as a 'link language', to quote a phrase used by Jawaharlal Nehru.

It might also be noted that of a little over 20,000 books published during 1965-66 in India, over 10,000 were in English, the rest distributed among the fourteen or more major national languages of the country. In some of them, like Assamese, the number was well below 100, and in Kashmiri not more than 10.

But apart from its utility as a language of higher education in the sciences and as a 'link language', English has also been voluntarily employed and is being so employed as a literary vehicle by a fair number of eminent Indians like Rammohun Roy, Vivekananda, Ranade, Gokhale, Aurobindo, Gandhi, Nehru, Radhakrishnan, and many others whose love of their land and its culture cannot be questioned. There has also been an almost uninterrupted stream of creative writing by Indians in this language, from Derozio in the 'twenties of the last century to R. K. Narayan today. Some even among the great pioneers of modern literature in Indian languages were tempted at the threshold of their career to adopt English as their creative medium, partly because they owed their inspiration to English literature and partly because they hoped thereby to reach a wider audience. Michael Madhusudan's first narrative poem, *The Captive Ladie,* and Bankim Chandra's early novel, *Raj-*

mohan's Wife, are classic examples.* The first modern poet in Marathi, Keshavsut, made early experiments in English verse, and the founder of modern Gujarati fiction, Govardhanram, has left behind his *Diaries* in English. Even Bharati who is hailed by many admirers as the most eloquent and patriotic among Indian poets was not averse to attempting both verse and prose in a foreign language, and among contemporary authors not a few have at one time or another tried their hand at creative expression in English. Wisely they discovered in time that they could create best in their own language.

Rabindranath Tagore whose patriotism was not of the kind to disown the debt that modern India owes to English language and literature was never tired of stressing, nonetheless, that no great or truly creative literature could be producd except in one's mother tongue. He was also the first among our educationists to insist that the child learns best through his mother tongue and had likened an exclusive reliance on English to the use of crutches which make a lot of clatter while the natural limbs get atrophied by disuse. In both these respects time and experience have amply justified Tagore's wisdom.

All the same, it is possible that Tagore overstressed the *mother tongue* aspect and did not perhaps adequately distinguish between a foreign language

* For an exhaustive survey of the whole field see Iyengar, K. R. Srinivasa, *Indian Writing in English*, Asia Publishing House, Bombay, 1962.

and a native or naturalised language of learning and culture which may not be one's mother tongue proper. This distinction is particularly relevant in a land where the mother tongues are very often dialects not normally employed as literary vehicles. It is doubtful if Sanskrit, as Panini standardised it, could ever have been the tongue in which Kalidasa or Jayadeva lisped to their mothers. Many distinguished writers of Hindi and Urdu—Premchand and Iqbal are illustrious examples—had to discard the dialects or speeches which were their mother tongues and adopted as their literary vehicles languages consciously cultivated for the purpose. Even today there are a number of noted poets and writers, Kaka Kalelkar in Gujarati, Bendre in Kannada, Yashpal, Balakrishna Rao and many others in Hindi, Krishan Chunder and Bedi in Urdu, born to one language and writing successfully in another of their adoption.

It might be more appropriate to say that if not necessarily the mother tongue proper, the language of one's cultural upbringing and environment is the best medium for creative expression. Such a language may even be foreign. How else explain the phenomenon of poets like Ghalib and Iqbal who wrote with equal facility and elegance in Persian and Urdu, and were, in fact, more proud of their vocation as Persian poets than as poets in Urdu? And yet Persian was no less foreign to India than English. Nor are such instances uncommon in the West. Joseph Conrad is justly honoured as an English writer, though he was born in

Ukraine of Polish parents and was 21 years old when he joined an English merchant ship. Many American writers were born in Russia, Germany, Italy, Poland or France and had to learn English and by no means at the mother's knee.

It is therefore hardly reasonable to belittle Indian writers who choose to write in English. In any case a writer has to be judged by the quality of his writing, irrespective of the medium he uses. Some novels of R. K. Narayan, a born story-teller with an eye for the odd and an enviable gift of gentle irony, are superior in intrinsic literary merit to a great deal of mediocre stuff that passes for literature in many Indian languages. On the other hand, it cannot be denied that so far as creative writing and in particular poetry is concerned, no Indian writing in English has reached anywhere near the heights attained by some of the great masterpieces in Indian languages. The testimony of Michael Madhusudan Dutt who was a great lover of European literature and was well-versed in many languages is worth recalling: 'Let those who feel that they have springs of fresh thought in them, fly to their mother tongue.'

What modern Indian literature lacks, and lacks sadly, is a well-proportioned and many-sided development. Rich in poetry and fiction (in particular short story), it is poor in drama, biography, in critical apparatus and the literature of knowledge in general. Though Indian life is full of contrast and conflict and therefore of drama (which, indeed, is being largely exploited in fiction, in scenarios for the screen and even in short radio-plays), drama as such has made little advance. Tagore's contribution to its indigenous development seems to have fallen like a rich seed in a barren field. What drama has been written and produced since is largely undistinguished, either leftist propaganda or patriotic ranting or blatant publicity of State welfare schemes, well-meaning but ill-conceived and ill-concealed, with little claim to literary or artistic merit. One of the reasons for this anaemic state is that drama has little scope for growth independently of the stage, and there is almost no professional stage worth the name in the cities of India, despite some brave experiments in Calcutta and elsewhere.

There is, indeed, no dearth of books written on literary research and criticism, but most of them are, unfortunately, if not actual theses submitted for University degrees, very much like such theses —laborious and unimaginative pedantry, little better than flogging the dead horse of Sanskrit poetics, or indiscriminate application of canons and isms borrowed from abroad irrespective of the Indian context and tradition, or, worse still, an unashamed boosting of national or regional claims.

Happily, this is not all. Despite the clamour of pedantry, of patriotic piety or political propaganda, good literature continues to be written in India, and as it vindicates itself it helps to sharpen the reader's sensibility. After all it is the creative writers who set the models on the basis of which critical standards and criteria grow up. And so, almost since the beginning of the present century, a growing minority of intelligent critics well-versed in the cultural traditions of their country and well-acquainted with the literary trends in the West have bravely maintained a wholesome approach that is neither overwhelmed by the burden of the past nor overawed by the glamour of the latest fashion. This healthy trend should gain in strength as the readers come to understand that in the republic of letters as in that of men, a sensitive and well-adjusted critical apparatus and its judicious and fearless exercise are the *sine qua non* of happy results.

In this respect, too, Tagore's was the most wholesome influence in modern Indian literature. Had he played up to the ultra-nationalist sentiment his great authority might have made the cultivation of a sane and balanced outlook difficult. 'In India what is needed more than anything else,' he wrote in a letter to Gilbert Murray,* 'is the broad mind which, because it is conscious of its own vigorous individuality, is not afraid of accepting truth from all sources.' To react to outside influence and to be capable of change was, as he repeatedly stressed, the privilege of life; to be impervious to influences from without was death. 'That modern Bengali poetry has drawn inspiration from European literature is beyond doubt. Some people find fault with it on that account and say that it is therefore not national. If it means that this kind of poetry is unnatural to Bengali taste, then it could hardly have grown in this soil, and if it had sprouted it should have withered in no time. There is as yet no such sign of withering.'†

If it is unwise to resist the new, it is no less unwise to assume that what we hail as modern is come to stay. 'The upsurge of the creative mind is not exhausted by any one seasonal crop. We may rest assured that another season will follow with its fresh harvest—how good or bad, time alone can assess. Man, say our scriptures, gives up his body of one birth to take up another in a new

* *East and West,* League of Nations, 1935.

† 'Adhunik Bangla Kabita': Rabindranath Tagore, *Kabi O Kabita,* 1965.

birth; in the same way his mind overrides the conventions of one age to get entangled in those of another. What it calls modern is only a new skin or coat which in course of time shall wear off. Age after age the life-spirit makes its own sheath and then breaks it asunder.' *

As regards the literature of knowledge, in particular the social and natural sciences, the position is indeed dismal, as may be seen from the data compiled by the National Library, Calcutta, for 1961-62. In the first place the total number of titles published (about 21,000) for a population of over 430 million works out at little more than 48 titles per million. In the second place 40 per cent of the titles published in India relate to literature, while only 4.5 per cent relate to science, and less than 1 per cent to technology and applied sciences. Although the position in the latter respect has since improved, the figures compare poorly with corresponding figures for most countries of the West as well as Japan, and indicate how much remains to be done before modern Indian literature as a whole gains a proper ballast.†

* *Ibid.*

† 'Current Publishing Trends in India' by C. R. Banerji, *Indian Literature*, Vol. V, No. 2, 1962, Sahitya Akademi, New Delhi. See also the same author's 'Indian Publishing: Recent Trends', also published in *Indian Literature*, Oct.-Dec. 1966, where he points out: 'Four years ago literature claimed the largest number of titles. But now social science group has taken the lead with 5137 titles. The next place is occupied by literature with 3121 volumes.'

What of the contemporary literary scene? One would imagine that the last Great War which shook the foundations of the modern world, and its aftermath, the attainment by India of Independence which changed the face of the land, would have had considerable impact on Indian literature. Unfortunately, no impact comparable to what was felt in the middle of the last century, or even in the two decades following the first World War in the present century, has been in evidence. So far as the intelligentsia was concerned, the Second War seemed merely to have aggravated the popular revulsion against insane violence and to have added to the growing disillusionment with the 'humane pretensions' of the Western world. This was eloquently voiced in Tagore's poems of the period and his last testament translated into English as *Crisis in Civilisation*.

The Indian intelligentsia was in a state of moral dilemma. On the one hand they had nothing but admiration for England's dogged courage in the hour of peril, they had much sympathy for Russia fighting with its back to the wall against the Nazi hordes, and for China groaning under the heel of Japanese militarism. On the other hand, their own country was, for all practical purposes, under military occupation of the very people who were resisting similar occupation of their own land. Added to it was the patriotic glamour of Subhas Bose and his insistent appeals to his countrymen to throw off the foreign yoke by any means. No creative upsurge could issue from such confusion of sympathies.

Strange as it may seem, even so revolutionary a change as the attainment of independence after centuries of chaos and subjection failed to release a proportionate upsurge of creative energy. No doubt, this long-hoped-for consummation of national aspirations was hailed with great enthusiasm and joy by the people, but this jubilation was soon submerged in the great agony of Partition with its insensate orgy of slaughter and the uprooting of millions of people from their homeland, followed by the martyrdom of Mahatma Gandhi. These tragedies, along with the invasion of Kashmir by tribal hordes from Pakistan, did indeed provoke a spate of poignant and fairly competent writing, particularly in the languages of regions directly affected, namely, Bengali, Punjabi, Kashmiri, Sindhi, Hindi and Urdu; but wails of anguish or thunder of curses or growls of anger do not by themselves turn into great literature.

If no great literature has as yet erupted from this chain of convulsions, it must be recalled that half a century had to elapse since Napolean's invasion of Russia before *War and Peace* was written, and that no literary monument comparable to Tolstoy's masterpiece has since been produced in Russian or in any language of the West, even though far greater horrors have been witnessed on their soil. What inspires great literature, and how and when it is produced, is a speculation which will continue to baffle literary historians. Is great literature produced when a people are beginning to awaken and dream of a great destiny or after they have awakened and achieved their destiny? At any rate Shakespeare, Goethe, Tolstoy and Tagore wrote when their people were awakening but had not yet fully awakened, when their aspirations were in making and nothing much had been achieved.

However, even if no great peaks are visible as once marked its landscape, Indian literature is richer today in volume, range and variety, the average level of writing is more competent and sophisticated, than it ever was in the past. The writers are exploring new fields and there is hardly a branch of literature in which experiments, some vigorous, are not being made. Translations from one Indian language into another as well as from many foreign languages have helped to widen both the writer's and the reader's horizon and to sharpen his critical sensibility. The Union and State Governments are increasingly aware of the role of literature in society and do what they can to encourage good writing, directly and through the

National and State Academies and Book Trusts.*

The number of writers who derive a comfortable income from their royalties, negligible twenty years ago, has risen rapidly. The readers' market, still deplorably poor, has nevertheless such vast potential that as illiteracy and poverty are eliminated and as the publishing industry is better organised, the Indian writer can confidently look forward to increasingly ample opportunities. To temper this optimism it is well to reflect that if economic prosperity and high literacy could by themselves produce great literature, the U.S. would be full of Shakespeares and the U.S.S.R. of Tolstoys.

Meanwhile, the contemporary literary scene is somewhat more blurred and confused than it was during the preceding decades of the modern period. To the long-standing antipathy between Traditionalists and Moderns have been added

---

* State patronage of literature is not without its dangers, inasmuch as it may encourage the production of a courtier-type of literature, servile and ornate. The number of poems, including epics, written on Jawaharlal Nehru in many Indian languages is legion. Not one has the beauty and intensity of feeling which Nehru's own brief tribute to Gandhi delivered extempore after the latter s assassination has. So too the State patronage of Hindi as the official language of the country has exposed the language to unhealthy influences. 'The Hindi platform,' writes Dr Nagendra, 'was so badly crowded by the politicians that the litterateurs were rudely elbowed out.' ('Trends in post-Independence Hindi Literature': Dr Nagendra, *Souvenir of the Fifth All India Writers' Conference, Kerala, 1965.*)

other factors which have deranged the earlier loyalties. Political wrangles and military skirmishes with China and Pakistan have inflamed the national ego, while the cold war among the great powers carried on mainly at the expense of small and helpless Asian countries has made the intelligentsia more sceptical than ever of the humanist slogans of the two blocks, democratic or communist. Since both systems represent two divergent developments of the same Western civilisation, and, however seemingly antithetical, are in truth two sides of the same coin, the virtues of Western civilisation as such, once held in high esteem, are being increasingly questioned and mocked.* Thus the invigorating climate of idealism and faith in which the modern period was born and nurtured is undergoing a radical change.

The earliest phase marked by an exhilaration of self-discovery and a romantic faith had gradually yielded to the pressure of objective realism coloured by national aspirations. The twentieth century saw the increasing impact in India of three major influences from the West—of Marx, Freud and experimental writing. These impacts were on the whole creative and led to a lively flowering of

---

* No less by Western intellectuals. 'Yet a man may have an impressive amount of mechanical ingenuity, sufficient to put other men into space, but behave like a spoilt child or a maniac in his personal life and be hypnotised by ideas that are wildly irrational.'—J. B. Priestley in an article on 'Growing Old' in *New Statesman*, 29 July 1966.

thought as well as a more impassioned or sophisticated, as the case may be, texture of writing. Today, however, the prevalent mood is one not of faith so much as of despair, not of daring as of defiance, not of passion as of morbidity. The sensitive ones among writers and poets are sombrely reflective or mildly apologetic; the blatant ones are loudly defiant, boisterously cynical or unashamedly obscene.

Perhaps a few specimens culled at random may help to illustrate. The first is from a recent published work of one of the more sensitive and intelligent of contemporary poets, Bishnu Dey: *

> I return home, scrape asphalt from sandals,
> wash the moist underwear, take bath
> > crow-fashion in cistern water.
> The garret is still hot as fire, the roof-tiles
> > melt
> in the heat of houses pressed one against
> > another;
> Yet what a relief to see smoke in the sky—
> everywhere in dust-bin Calcutta's warehouses
> > the eyes burn.
> No, no summer storm—cloud, wind, tempest,
> > sea,
> all dead these days, however much of an
> > optimist I may be deep down.
> And so in dulled consciousness I doze all
> > alone on this tiny slice of a roof,

* Dey, Bishnu, *Sei Andhakar Chai*, Bharabi, Calcutta, 1966. English translation by Dr Lokenath Bhattacharya.

wake up only when called to eat. Is that
                              the rain, frantic, delirious ?
In my heart too waken the clouds, the wind
              and the thunder's heartening rumble—
and awakens too the melodic note, wistful,
                  joyous, of Tagorean loveliness
as roof to roof the blue showers of rain
                              descend on the body.

Here is a different mood, of sarcasm, from a no
less distinguished modern Hindi poet, with very
different political sympathies :

Snake, you were never civilised,
And you never learned
How to live in the city.
I'd like to ask—(if you'll answer)—
How, then, did you learn to bite—
Where did you get the poison? *

And one of mockery by an angry Tamil poet:

Introduced to
the Upanishads
by T. S. Eliot;

and to Tagore
by the earlier
Pound;

* By 'Ajneya'. Indian Literature Number of *Sameeksha*,
December 1965. English rendering by the author (S. H.
Vatsyayan) and L. E. Nathan.

and to the Indian
tradition by
Max Mueller
(late of the Bhavan);

and to the Indian
dance by
Bowers;

and to the Indian
art by
what is his name

and to the Tamil
classics by Danielou
(was he Pope?);

Flesh nor fish
blood nor bone
totempole;

vociferous in
thoughts not
his own;

eloquent in
words not
his own
(the age demanded. . .) *

* By Ka Naa Subramanyam. English translation by the
poet. Published in *Sameeksha,* December 1965.

Yet another, even more angry and unrestrained :

> There is a drop of blood at the tip of my pen—
> Take, Oh, take it away!
> Wash your gods in it,
> Baptise your parents,
> And go down the Fallopian drain!
>
> And with this round little red
> Make the lunar disc a little more pink;
> So our solar system may stink
> —Let bloody Brahma wink! *

And an angry poet from Bengal, not to be left behind :

> This time I shall push on
> across the electrified barbed wire
> which barricades your ovary
> in my cerebellum floats the image
> of my mother's agonised face
> as of 2nd November 1939
> the flowing tides of the Hooghly
> surge back with the fecund earth
> fashioned out of the ashes
> of my unknown forebears
> and yet I go on feeding
> the fire of my sperm
> let it be fertilised in your ovary
> let me be given

* By Kerala poet Ayyappa Panicker. English translation by the poet. *Ibid.*

> my pen and ink and paper
> and seal and wax
> inside the ovary.*

Such defiant flaunting of sex is the very opposite of the erotic tradition in Indian poetry. This tradition was amorous, not obscene; it rejoiced and not squirmed in sex; it was playful and tender even in passion, never morbid and hateful as in despair. Having lost our moorings in the indigenous lore we are obliged to borrow the foreign fashion which, despite the Freudian insights, is so crude that the modern gloating over sex is invariably accompanied by a sense of guilt or disgust if it is secretive, and by an air of bravado and originality if it is brazen. What was a legitimate and playful enjoyment to the forefathers has become a morbid and guilty excitement to the progeny.†

---

* By Malay Rai Choudhury. Published in the periodical, *Krittibas*. English translation by Kshitis Roy.

† Although the main inspiration for this kind of defiant sex-gloating has been derived from a current Western fashion, this does not mean that the best minds of Europe and America are not critical of this aberration. 'Why, by the way,' asks Eric Bentley in a letter to the Editor, *Evergreen Review*, June 1966, 'should originality be considered praiseworthy? In many matters, may be including sex, it can be good to be *un*original. In any case, the burden of proof would be on the champion of originality. After reading all the stupid stuff you publish in favour of sex, one longs for some highly puritanical reading matter, written by non-morons.'

Fortunately, poetry is so unlike politics that the louder a poet screams the less he is heard. And so most of these angry poets, repetitive in originality and trivial in audacity, have a very limited audience mostly confined to coteries of mutual back-clappers. Not long ago, on the anniversary of Tagore's birth in May 1966, two new and unusual poetry journals were launched in Calcutta with a great bang of publicity, *Dainik Kabita* (Daily Poetry) and *Kabita-Ghantiki* (Poetry Hourly), the latter releasing an issue every hour. Needless to say, they soon petered out with a whimper, the Poetry Hourly not even lasting twelve hours. The Daily Poetry lasted a few days and carried in one of its issues an apt verdict on itself in the words of a distinguished literary critic: 'When Guru Eliot discovered the modern poetic wasteland, he didn't foresee that bits and pieces of it could produce murder more foul than that perpetrated in the Cathedral. Much of recent poetry, English and Bengali, is murderous indeed, mangled heaps of words, communicating little sound, sense much less. Much of recent Bengali poetry is uncreative and decreative.' *

More than forty years earlier Tagore had warned against the glamour of such aberrations perpetrated in the name of originality : 'Our modern mind, a hasty tourist in the rush over the miscellaneous, ransacks cheap markets of curios which mostly are delusions ... She racks her resources in order to be striking ... The same herd instinct is followed in a cult of rebellion as it was in the cult of conformity, and the defiance, which is a mere counteraction of obedience, also shows obedience in a defiant fashion.' †

* Saroj Acharya in *Dainik Kabita*, 15th issue, May 24, 1966. In this connection the following poem by a young Bengali poet, Lokenath Bhattacharya, might serve to illustrate the reaction in a sensitive mind to the plethora of trivial versifying:

The sky is there, yes, the orange sun is there. But there is no more poetry in life, nor in mind—only the tyranny of shallow versifiers terrorises. Herds of donkeys have their long ears moving in the wind. Deceitful, vain, garrulous donkeys—cut their impotent genitals off with a pair of enormous scissors!
Better is the still night, even the speechless no-dawn of despair. O God, give us silence, hush these versifiers and that loudspeaker at Beadon Square!
O God give us compassion to love our brothers, give our brothers compassion to love us, give the mind's nostrils the smell of purity—poetry may come later!

(The original Bengali text published in *Purbasha*, 1965.)

† 'The Religion of an Artist': A Lecture delivered in China in 1924. Published by Visva-Bharati, Calcutta, 1953.

The odd always attracts more notice than the normal. It would be misleading if the few specimens quoted earlier were interpreted as summing up the contemporary phase, or a dominant aspect, of modern Indian literature. Far from it. The main contours and features of the landscape remain what they were, despite the dust raised by a few shifting undulations here and there. For modern Indian literature is not a mushroom growth of exotic plants in a native wilderness. It is an ancient cultivation drawing its sustenance from a well-worn but rich soil to which many streams have periodically brought their alluvial deposits and on which many winds have scattered seeds brought from far and near. To all these streams and winds—the latest has come from the West with its main fertilising agent the English language—Indian literature owes a debt and has offered its welcome and hospitality.

A thousand varieties transplanted from distant soils have enriched the Indian flora. Nevertheless, the ancient lotus continues to bloom and to claim allegiance as the Indian flower *par excellence.* Even so, despite the changing pattern of Indian literature, from age to age, and from language to language, some strands have proved more characteristic than others and have persisted through the ages. One of them—an intense awareness of the Ultimate—has, like the snow-clad Himalayas, never ceased to dominate the Indian landscape.

More than 3,000 years ago the poet of a *Rig Veda* hymn wondered whence and how this creation arose when there was neither non-being nor being in the primeval nothingness. 'Whether He has made it or whether He has not, He who is the Overseer of the Universe in the highest heaven, He alone knows, or perhaps, even He does not know.' Lying in his sick bed, barely 12 days before his death, Tagore, unable to sit up or hold a pen, dictated the following testament :

> The first day's Sun
> asked
> at the new manifestation of being—
> Who are you?
> No answer came.
> Year after year went by,
> the last Sun of the day
> the last question utters
> on the western seashore
> in the silent evening—
> Who are you?
> He gets no answer.*

* *Poems*, Visva-Bharati, Calcutta, 1942. The English translation is by Amiya Chakravarty.

general

1. *Linguistic Survey of India* (20 Vols.). Government of India, 1903-28.
2. *Languages and Literatures of Modern India*: Suniti Kumar Chatterji. Bengal Publishers, Calcutta, 1963.
3. *Indian Literature*: A Symposium edited by Dr Nagendra. Lakshmi Narain Agarwal, Agra, 1959.
4. *Contemporary Indian Literature*: A Symposium, Sahitya Akademi, New Delhi, 1959 (2nd ed.).
5. *The Gazetteer of India*, Vol. I. Publications Division, Government of India, New Delhi, 1965.

language-wise

1. *History of Assamese Literature*: Birinchi Kumar Barua. Sahitya Akademi, New Delhi, 1964.
2. *Studies in the Literature of Assam*: Surya Kumar Bhuyan. Lawyers' Book Stall, Gauhati, 1956.
3. *History of Bengali Literature*: Sukumar Sen, Sahitya Akademi, New Delhi, 1960.
4. *History of Bengali Language and Literature*: Dinesh Chandra Sen, University of Calcutta, 1954.
5. *Bengali Literature*: J. C. Ghosh. Oxford University Press, London, 1948.

6. *Cultural Heritage of Bengal*: Romesh Chunder Dutt. Punthi Pustak, Calcutta, 1962 (3rd revised edition).
7. *The Bengali Drama—Its Origin and Development*: P. Guha-Thakurta. Kegan Paul, Trench, Trubner, London, 1930.
8. *An Acre of Green Grass*: Buddhadev Bose. Orient Longmans, Calcutta, 1948.
9. *Indian Writing in English*: K. R. Srinivasa Iyengar. Asia Publishing House, Bombay, 1962.
10. *Milestones in Gujarati Literature*: K. M. Jhaveri. K. M. Jhaveri, Bombay, 1914.
11. *Further Milestones in Gujarati Literature*: K. M. Jhaveri. K. M. Jhaveri, Bombay, 1924.
12. *The Modern Vernacular Literature of Hindustan*: G. A. Grierson. Asiatic Society, Calcutta, 1889.
13. *A History of Hindi Literature*: K. B. Jindal. Kitab Mahal, Allahabad, 1955.
14. *A History of Hindi Literature*: F. E. Keay, Y.M.C.A. Publishing House, Calcutta, 1960.
15. *A History of Kanarese Literature*: E. P. Rice. Y.M.C.A. Publishing House, Calcutta, 1921.
16. *History of Kannada Literature*: R. S. Mugali. Sahitya Akademi, New Delhi (English ed. in preparation).
17. *History of Kashmiri Literature*: J. L. Kaul. Sahitya Akademi, New Delhi (to be published shortly).
18. *A History of Maithili Literature* (2 Vols): J. K. Mishra. Allahabad, 1949-1950.
19. *History of Malayalam Literature*: P. K. Parameswaran Nair, Sahitya Akademi, New Delhi, 1967.
20. *A Short History of Marathi Literature*: M. K. Nadkarni. Baroda, 1921.
21. *History of Modern Marathi Literature* (1800-1938): G. C. Bhate. Poona, 1939.
22. *History of Oriya Literature*: Mayadhar Mansinha. Sahitya Akademi, New Delhi, 1962.
23. *Modern Oriya Literature*: P. R. Sen. University of Calcutta, 1947.

24. *A History of Punjabi Literature*: Mohan Singh. Lahore, 1931.

25. *History of Indian Literature*, Vol. I, Part I (Introduction and Veda): M. Winternitz. University of Calcutta, 1959.

26. *History of Indian Literature*, Vol. III, Part I (Classical Sanskrit): M. Winternitz. Motilal Banarsidas, Delhi, 1963.

27. *A History of Sanskrit Literature*: A. B. Keith. Oxford University Press, London, 1920 (Reprint 1956).

28. *A History of Sanskrit Literature* (Classical Period), Vol. I.: S. N. Dasgupta. University of Calcutta, 1947.

29. *History of Sindhi Literature*:   L. H. Ajwani. Sahitya Akademi, New Delhi (to be published shortly).

30. *Shah Abdul Latif of Bhit*:   H. T. Sorley. Oxford University Press, London, 1940.

31. *History of Tamil Language and Literature*: Vaiyapuri Pillai. New Century Book House, Madras, 1956.

32. *A History of Tamil Literature*: Jesudasan and H. Jesudasan. Y.M.C.A. Publishing House, Calcutta 1961.

33. *Telugu Literature*: P. T. Raju. P.E.N., Bombay, 1944.

34. *History of Telugu Literature*: G. V. Seethapathy. Sahitya Akademi, New Delhi (in press).

35. *A History of Urdu Literature*: Ram Babu Saxena. Allahabad, 1927.

miscellaneous *(referred to in the text)*

1. *The Foundations of Indian Culture*: Sri Aurobindo. Sri Aurobindo Library, New York, 1953.

2. *Glimpses of Medieval Indian Culture*: Yusuf Hasain. Asia, Bombay, 1957.

3. *A Bunch of Old Letters*: Asia Publishing House, Bombay, 1958.

4. *Census of India 1961*, Vol. I. Government of India, Delhi, 1964.
5. *Leaves from the Jungle: Life in a Good Village*: Verrier Elwin. John Murray, London, 1936.
6. *Ancient Indians Erotics and Erotic Literature*: S. K. De. Firma K. L. Mukhopadhyay, Calcutta, 1959.
7. *India Wins Freedom*: Abul Kalam Azad. Orient Longmans, India, 1959.
8. *Brochure on Printing*: National Library, Calcutta, 1956.
9. *Iqbal, His Art and Thought*: Sayed Abdul Vahid. Shaikh Md. Ashraf, Lahore, 1944.
10. *East and West*: League of Nations, 1935.
11. *The Religion of an Artist*: A Lecture delivered by Rabindranath Tagore in China, 1924. Visva-Bharati, Calcutta, 1953.
12. *Poems*: Rabindranath Tagore. Visva-Bharati, Calcutta, 1942.
13. *Bharati in English Verse*: S. Prema, Madras, 1958.
14. *Prem Chand—His Life and Work*: Hans Raj 'Rahbar'. Atma Ram & Sons, Delhi, 1957.
15. *Interpretations of Ghalib*: J. L. Kaul. Atma Ram & Sons, Delhi, 1957.
16. *British Policy in India* 1858-1905. S. Gopal, Cambridge University Press, 1965.
17. *Indian Literature*: Quarterly Journal, Sahitya Akademi, New Delhi. Vols. I-IX.